Welcome to a vibrant world of feathered wonders! This coloring book invites you to embark on a captivating journey through the enchanting realm of avian beauty. Immerse yourself in the intricate details of these majestic creatures, each page offering a canvas for your creativity to take flight. From the brilliant plumage of tropical parrots to the graceful soar of eagles, discover the diverse and stunning array of birds that grace our skies. Grab your colored pencils and let the colors burst forth, transforming these black-and-white illustrations into a kaleidoscope of hues. Get ready to bring these avian wonders to life and make this coloring experience soar to new heights!

Ricardo Silveira

2024

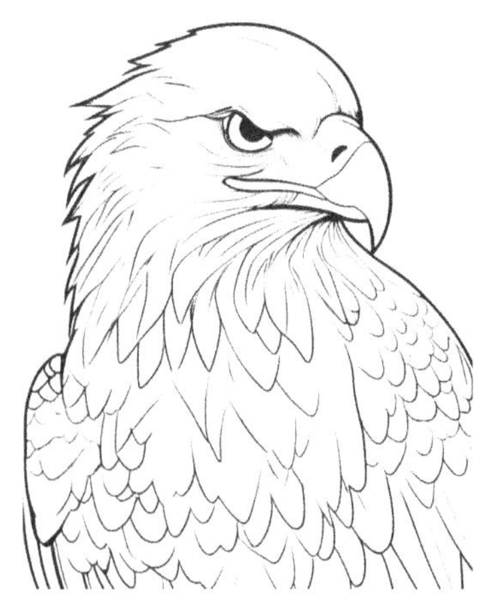

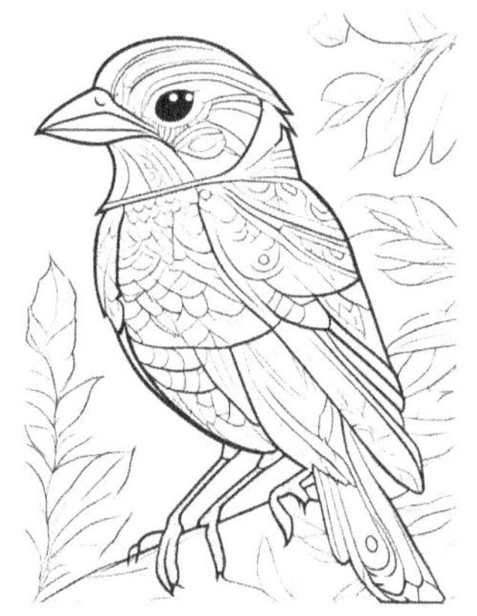

This Book Belongs to:

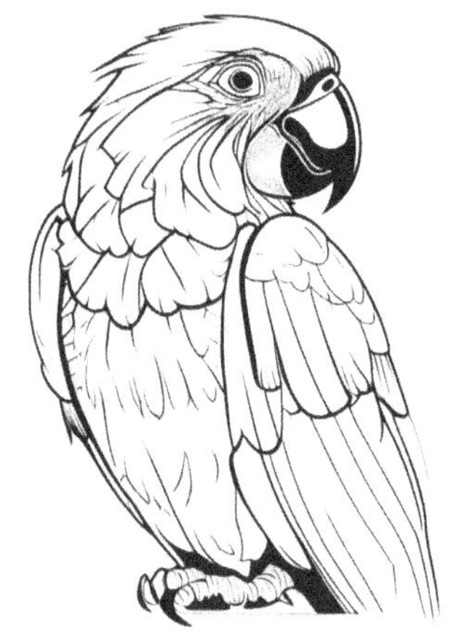

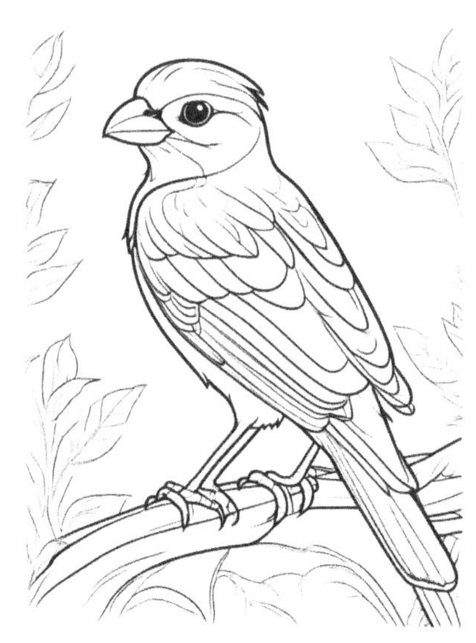

Test Color Page

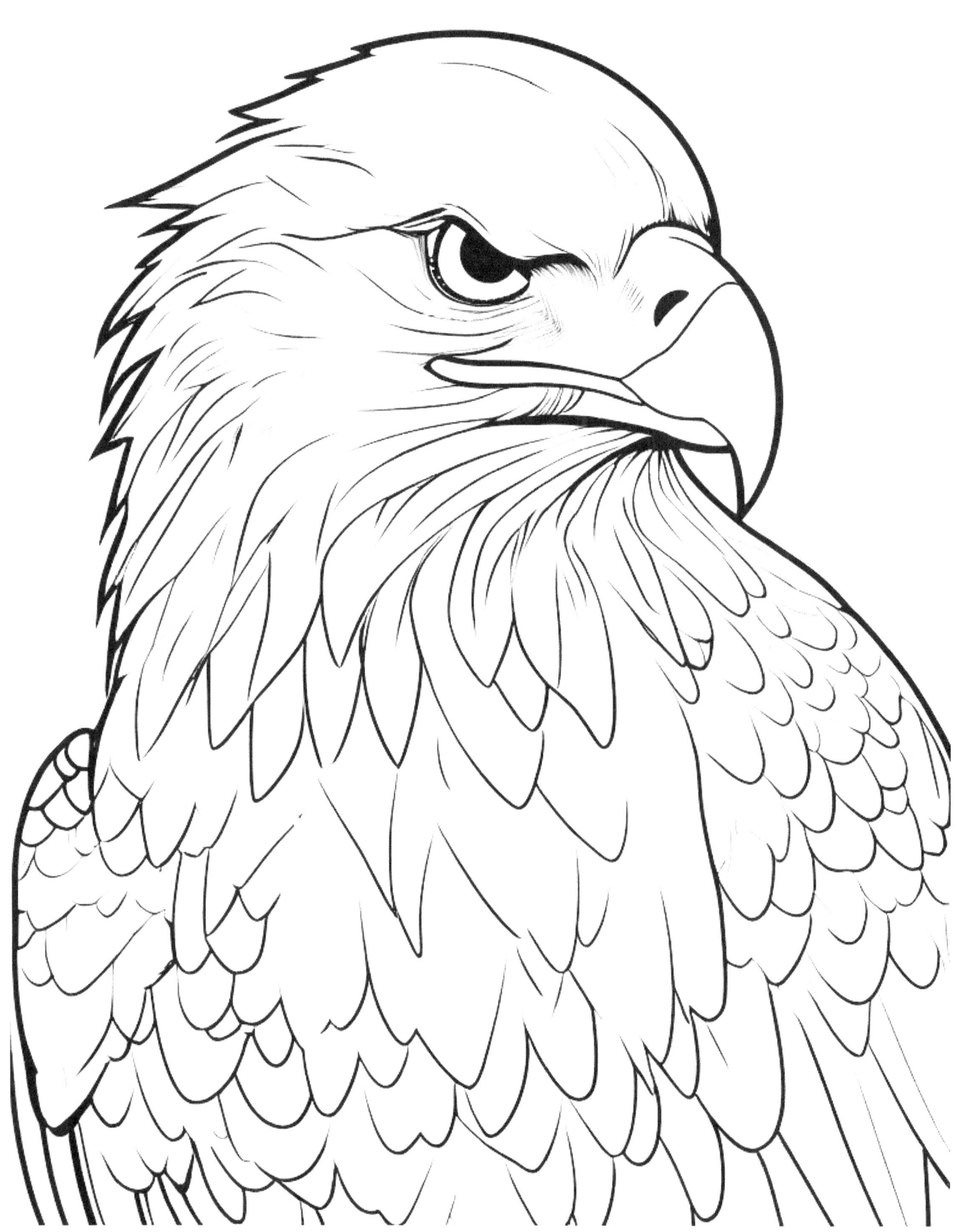

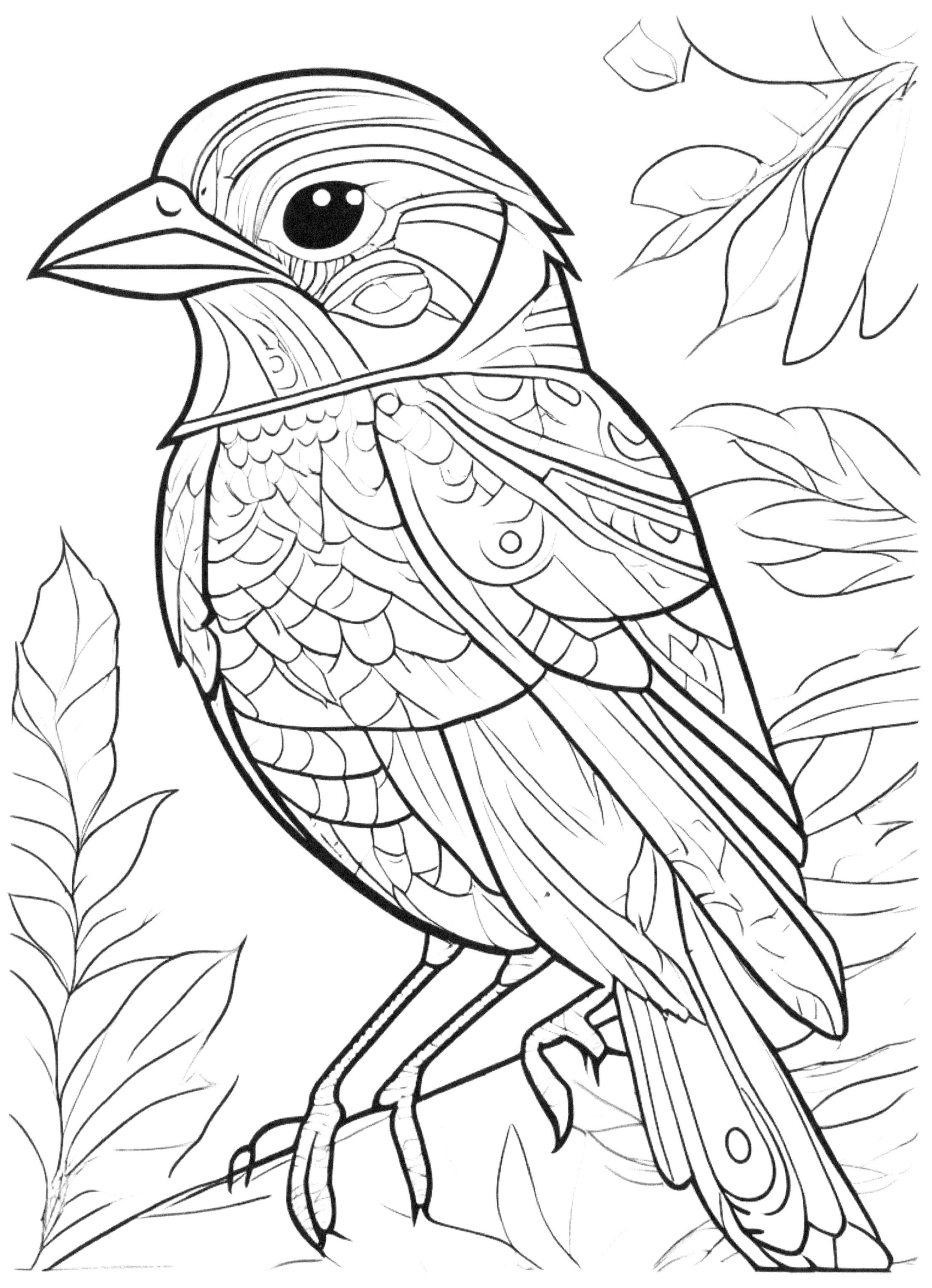

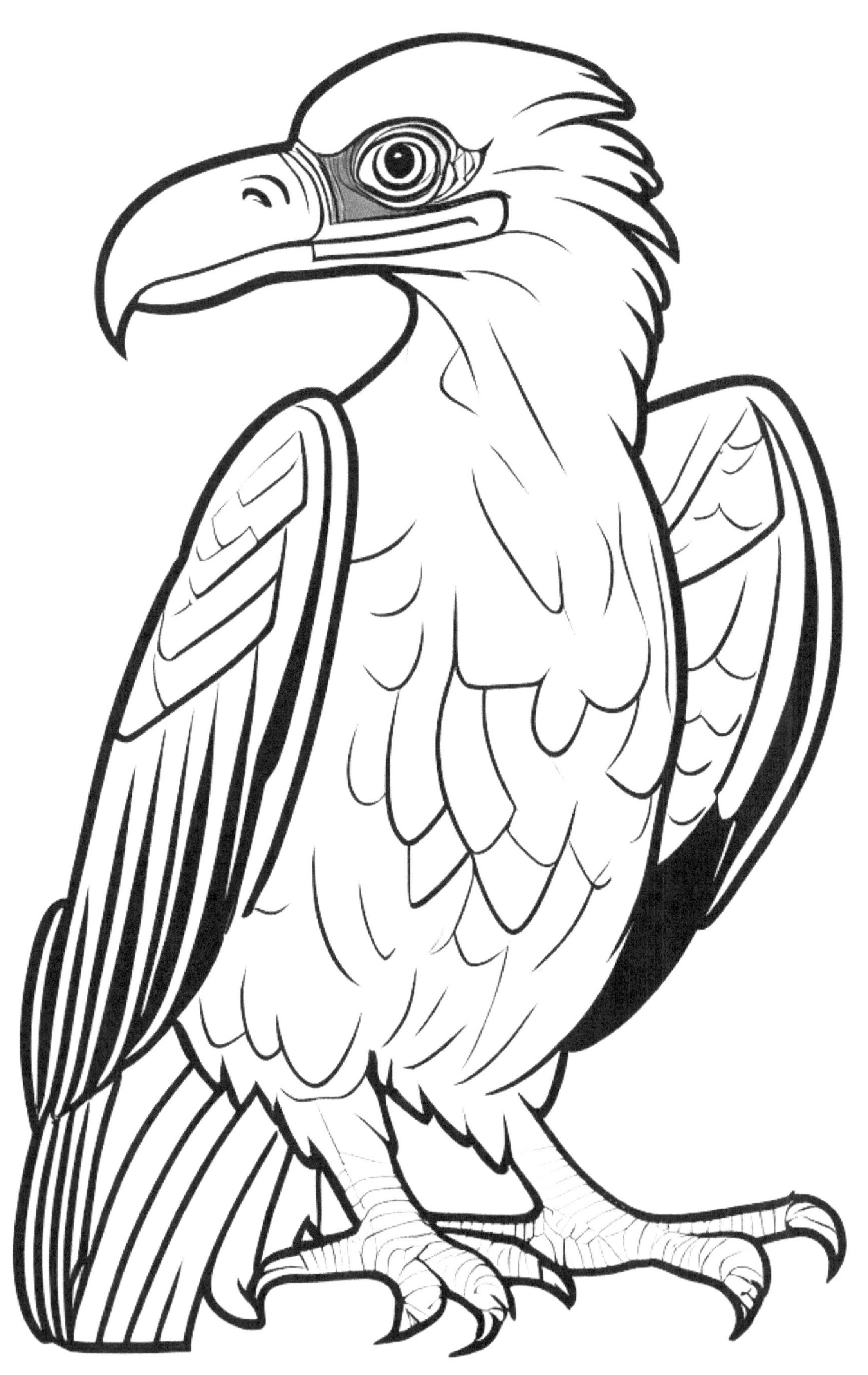

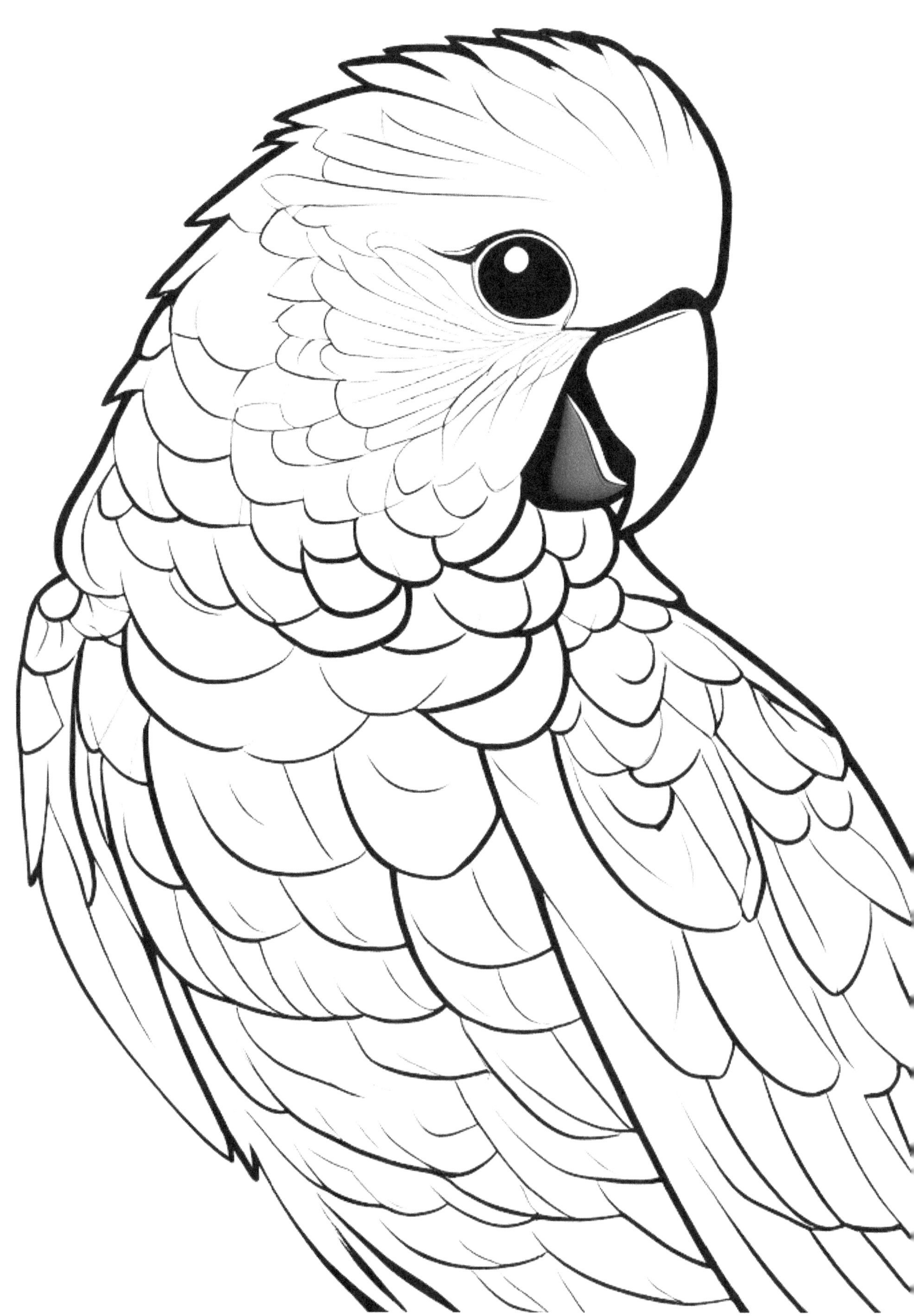

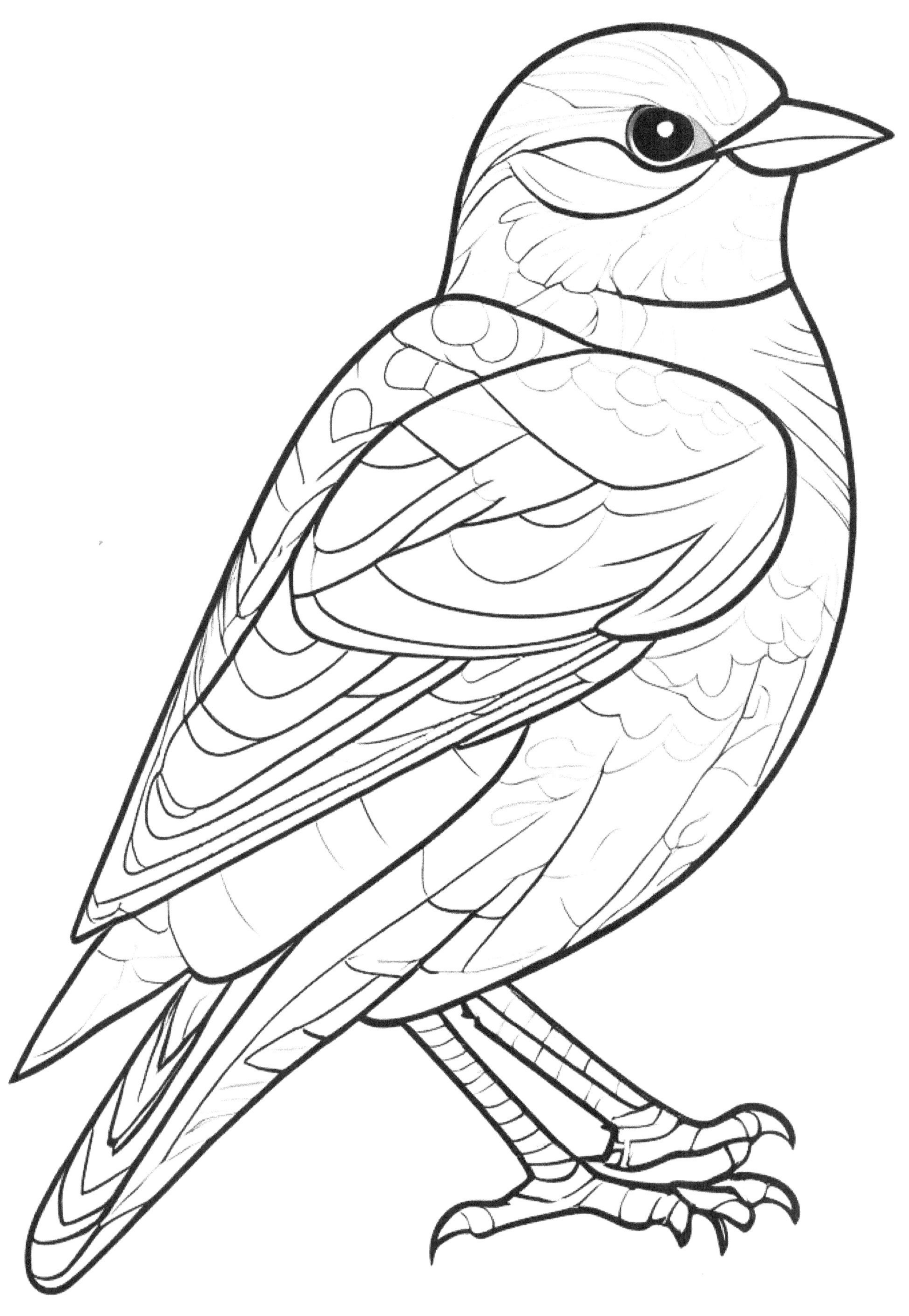

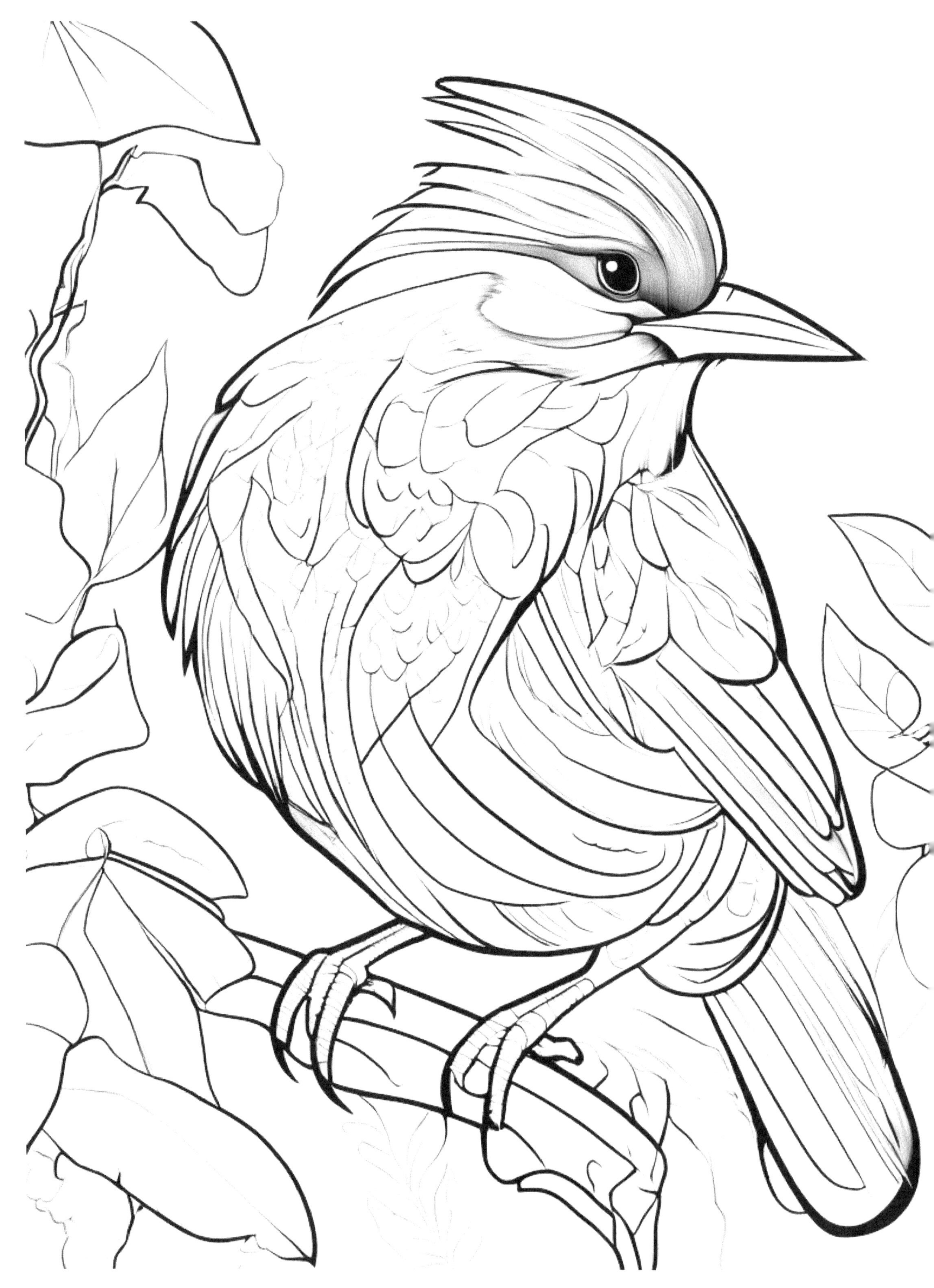

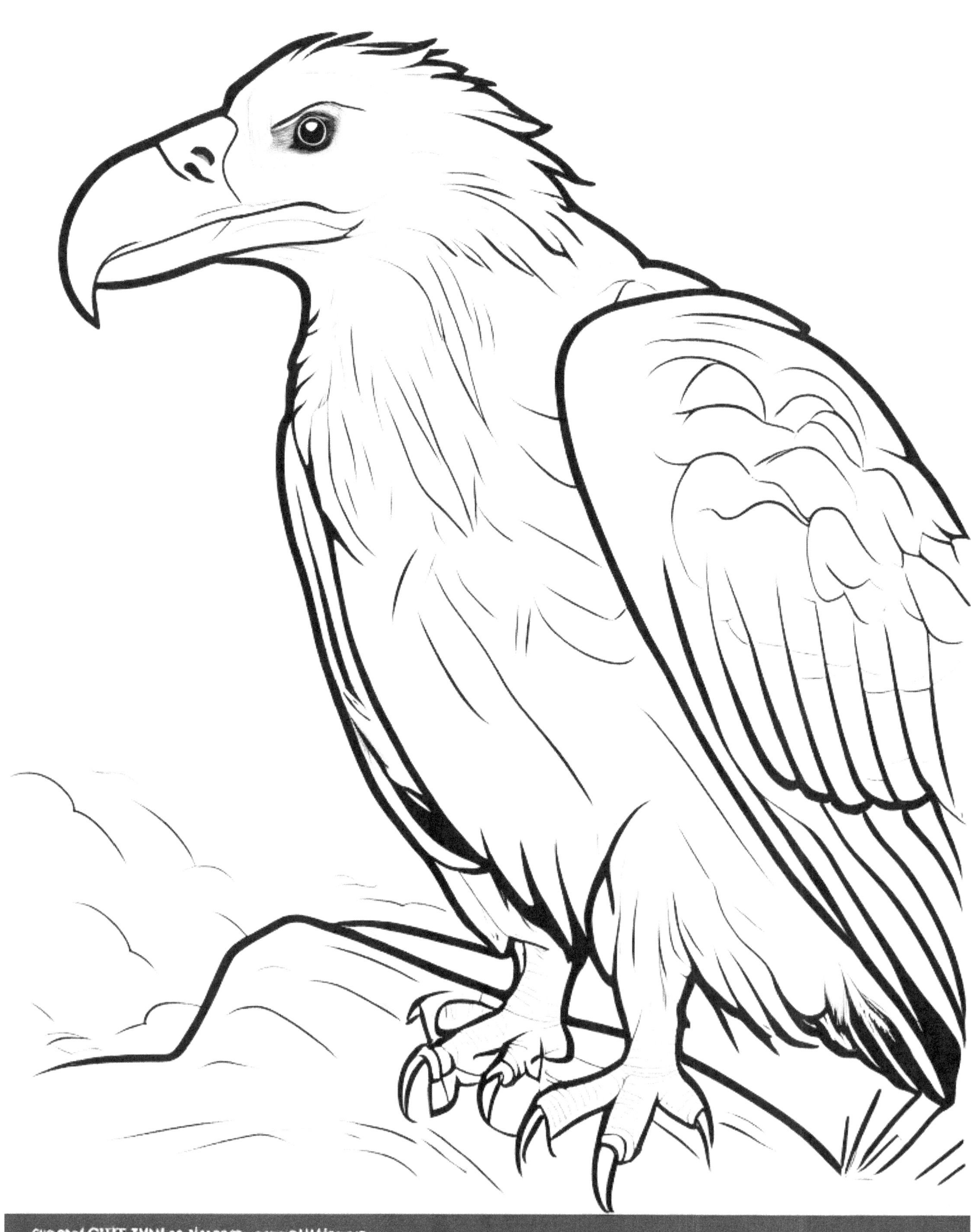

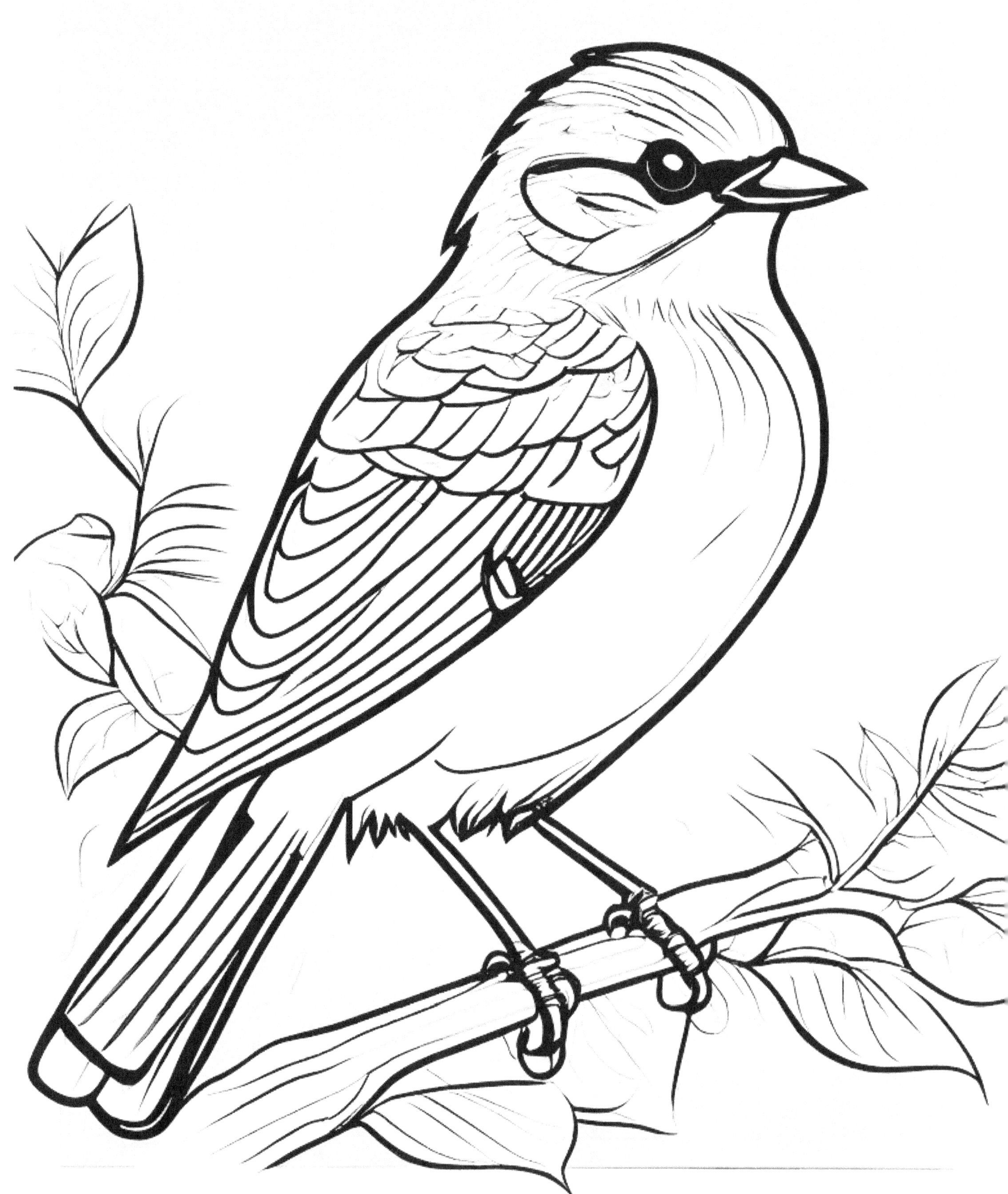

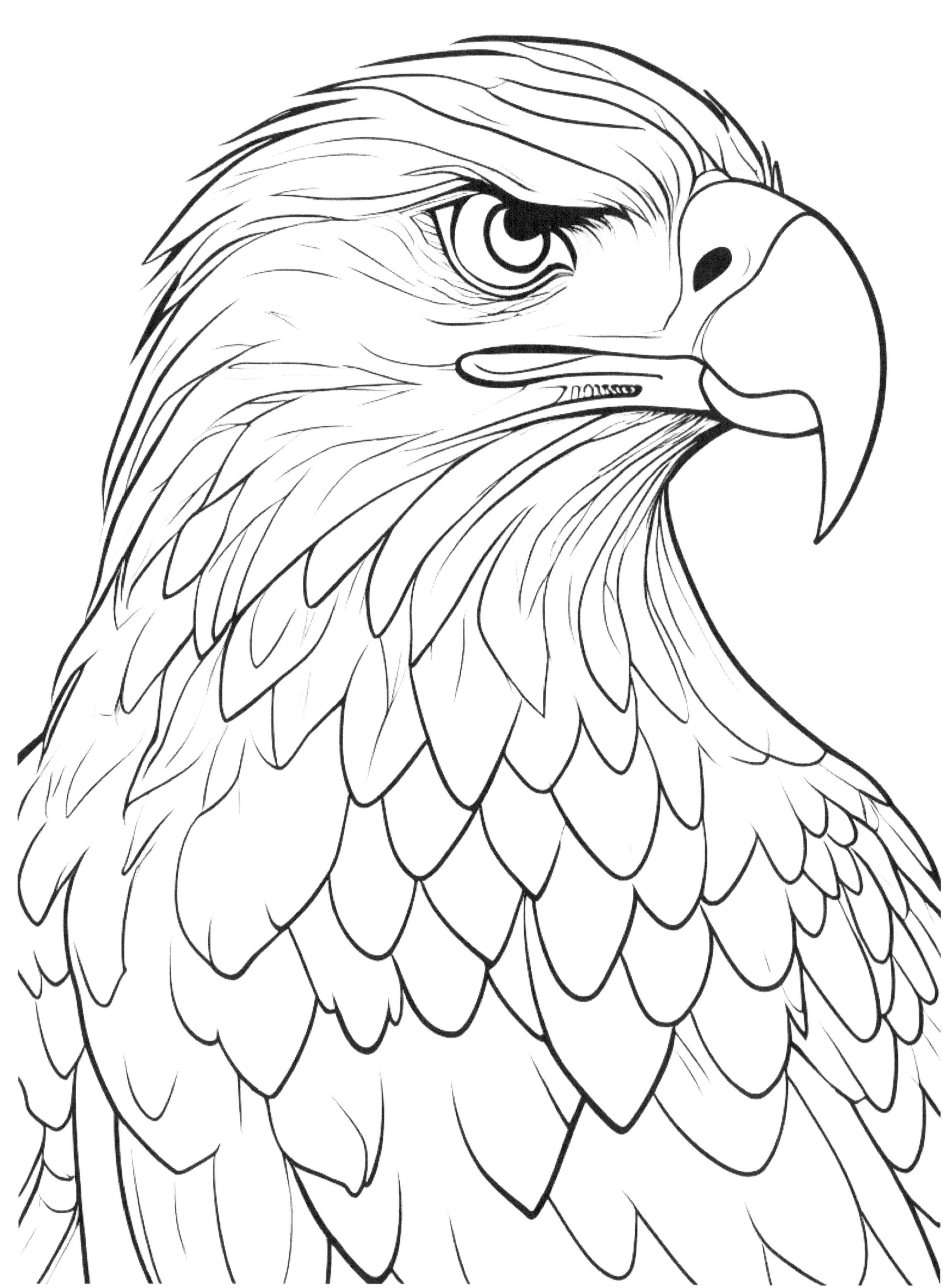

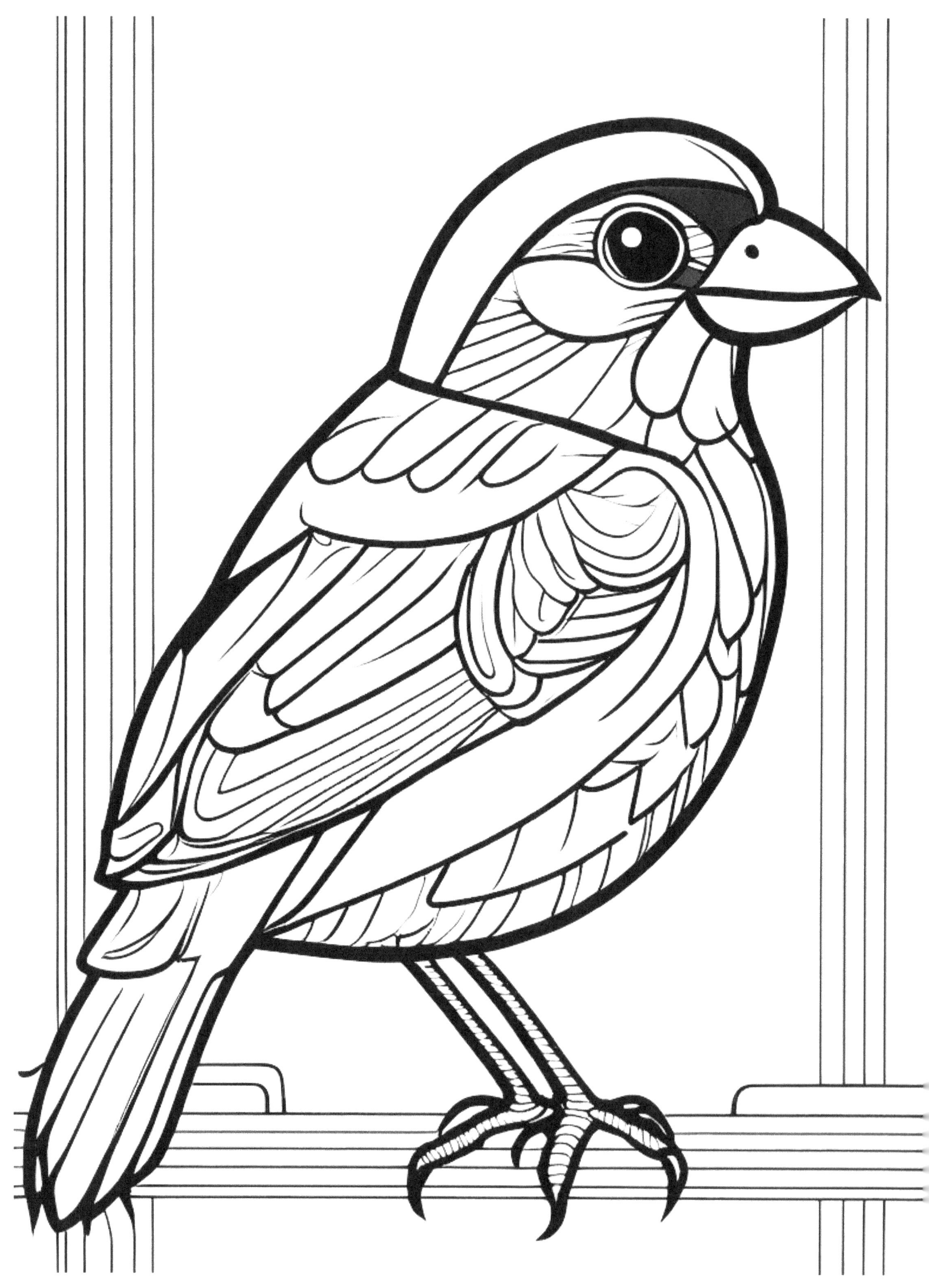

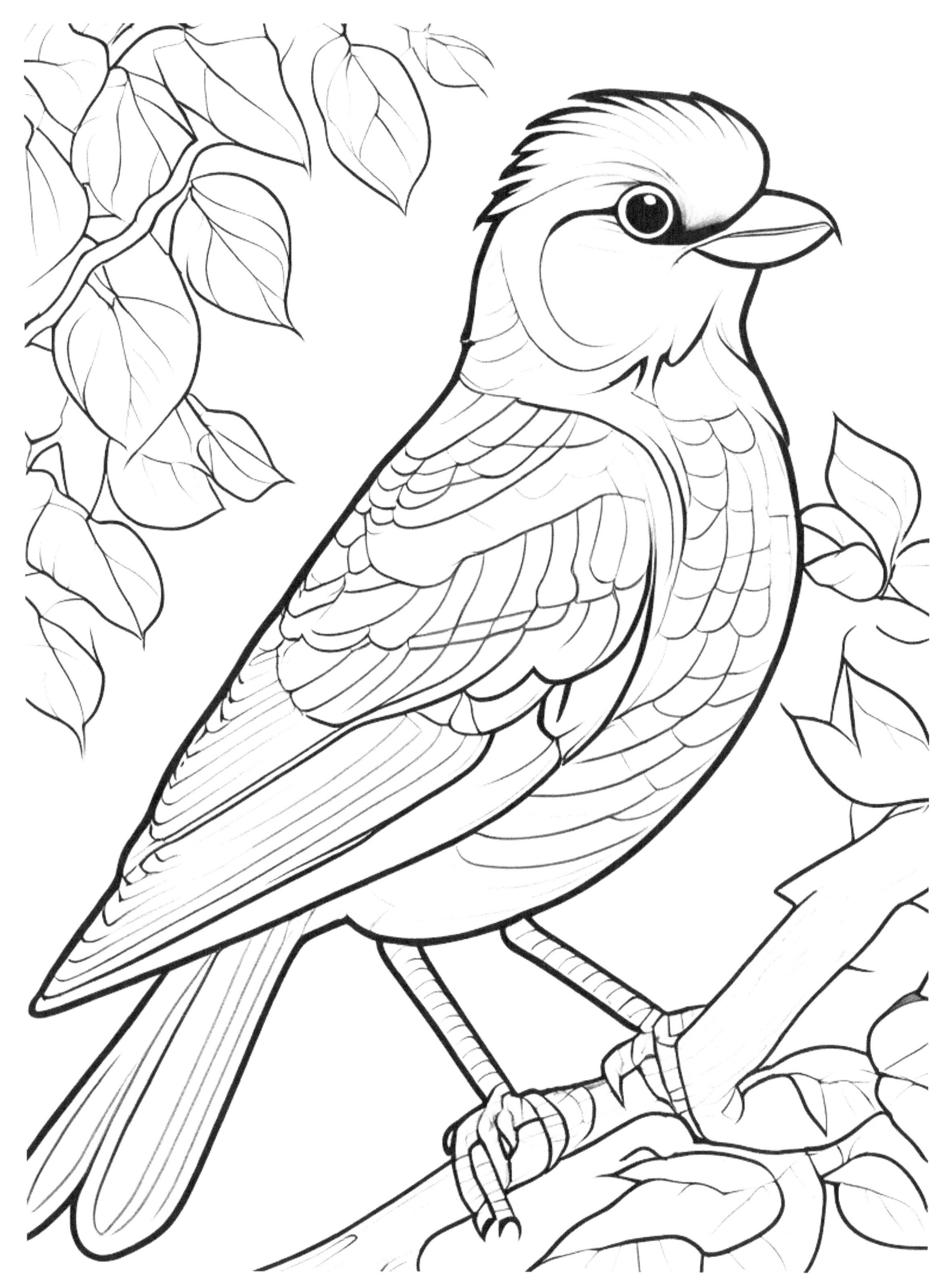

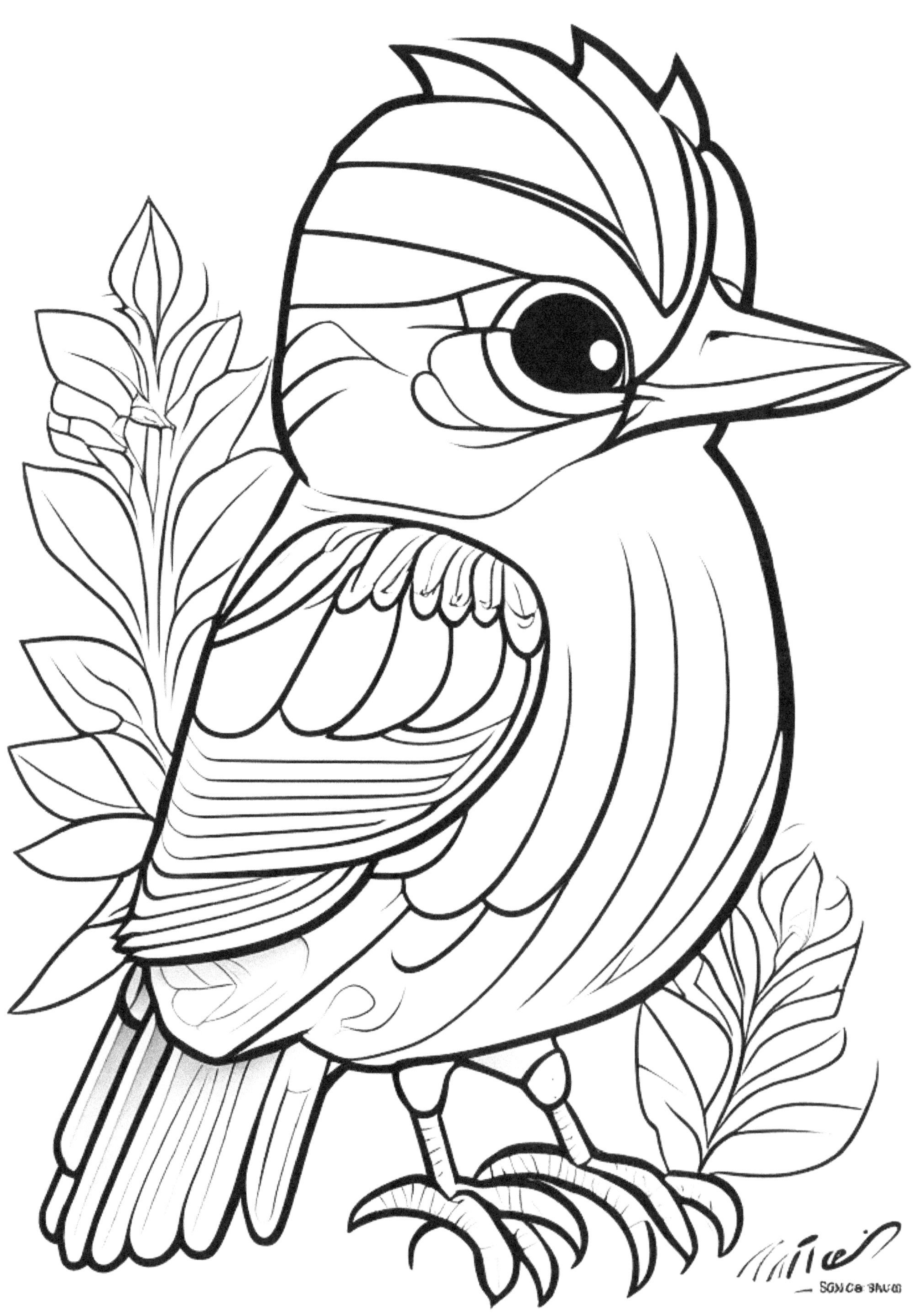

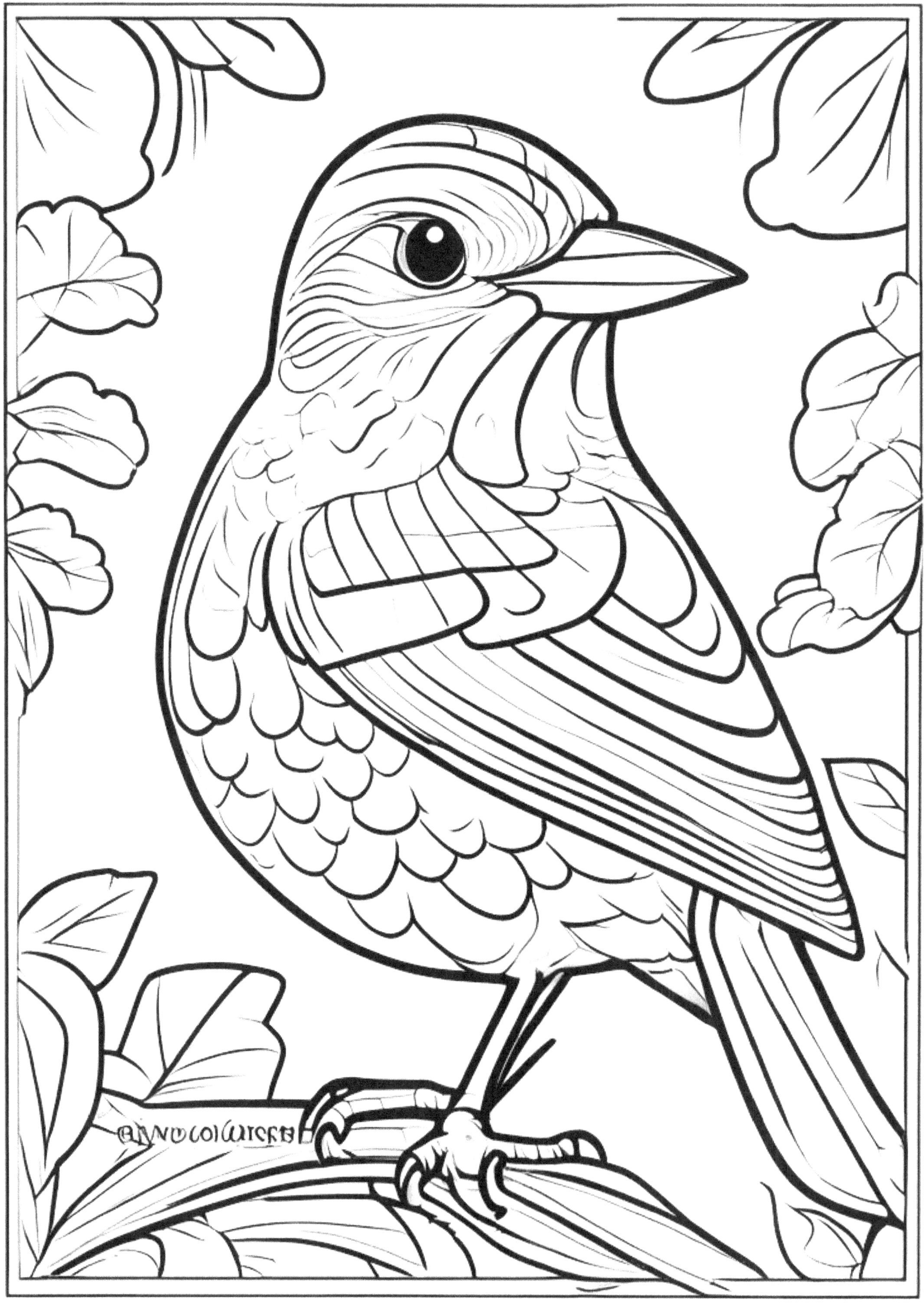

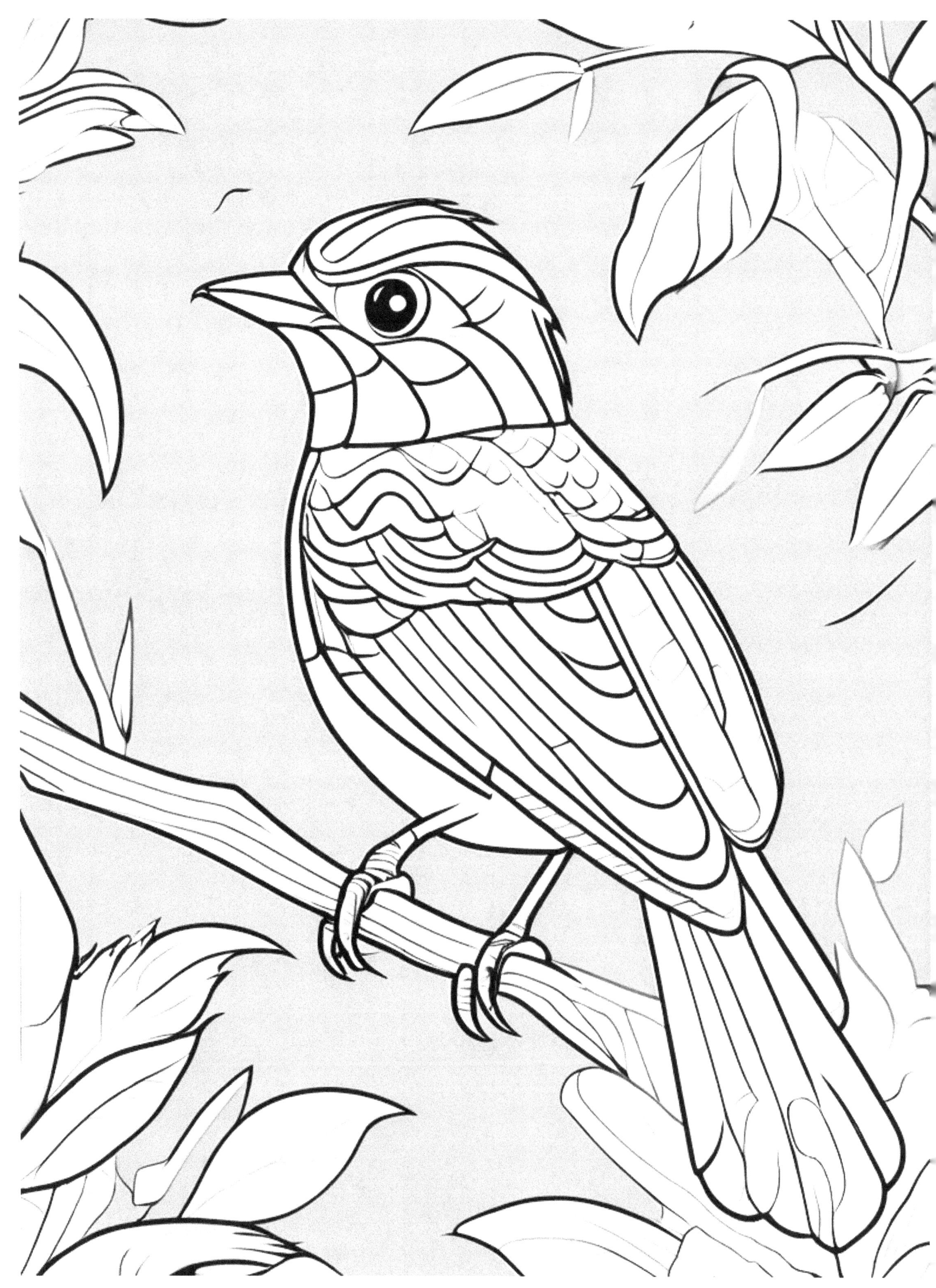

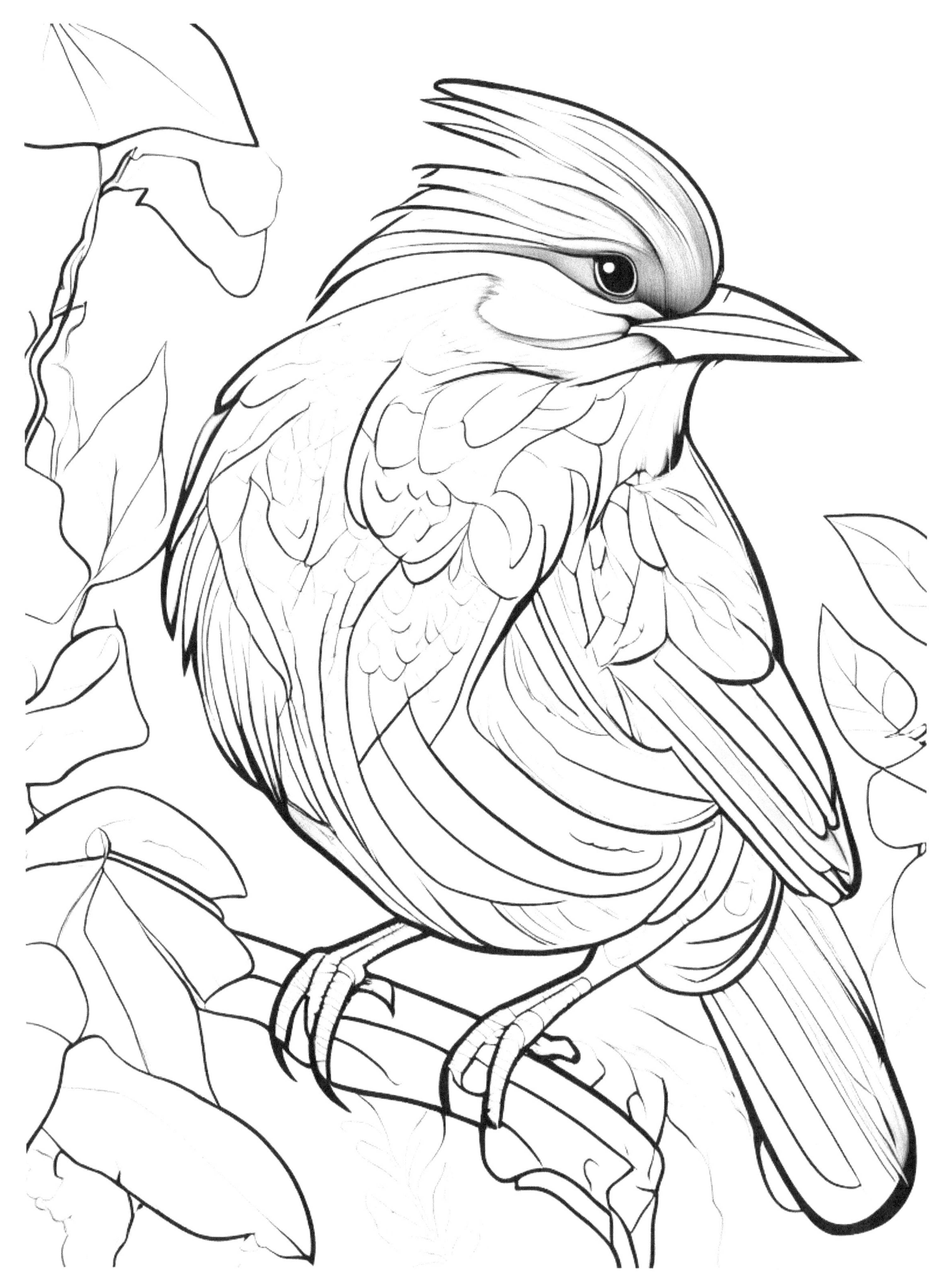

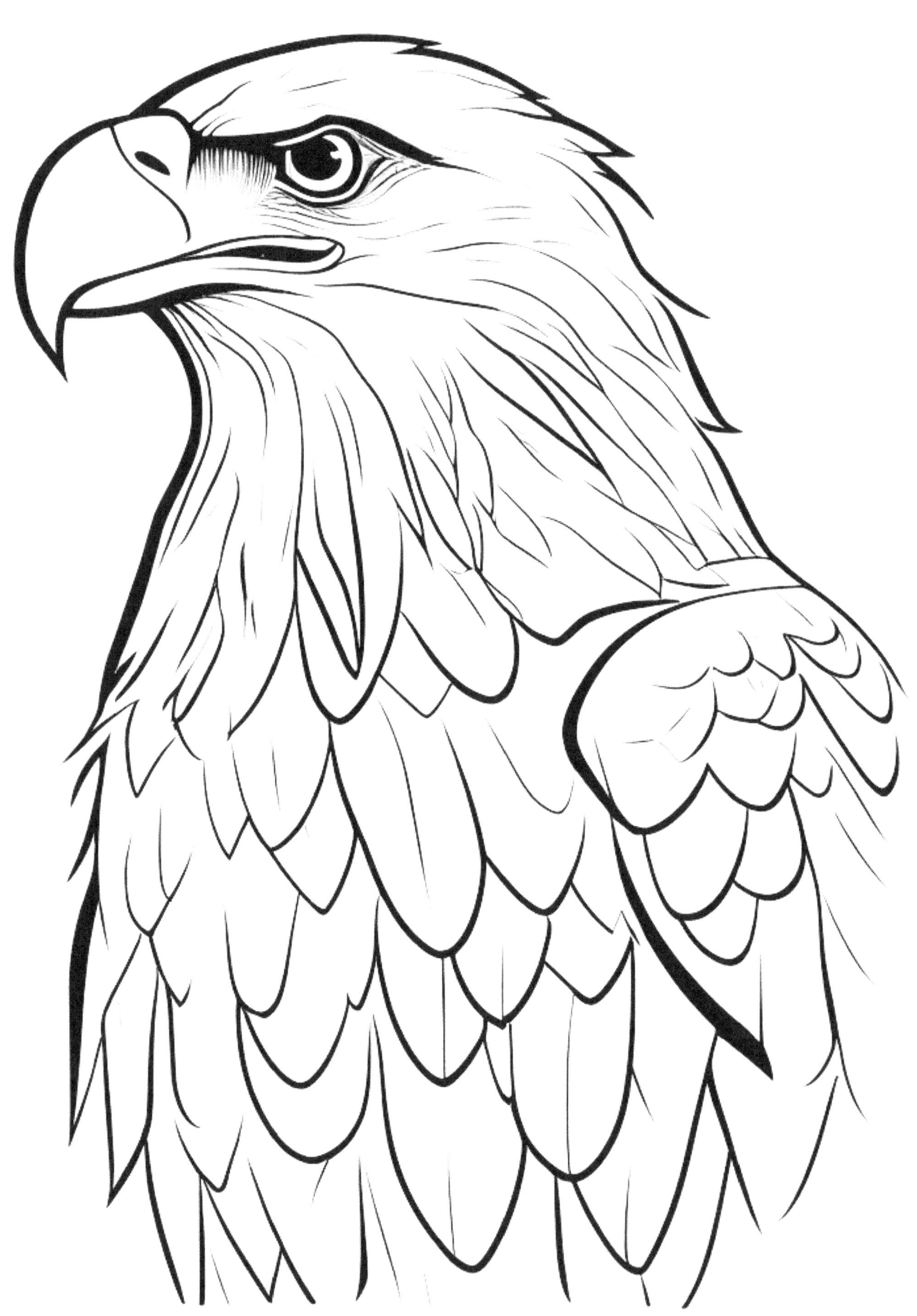

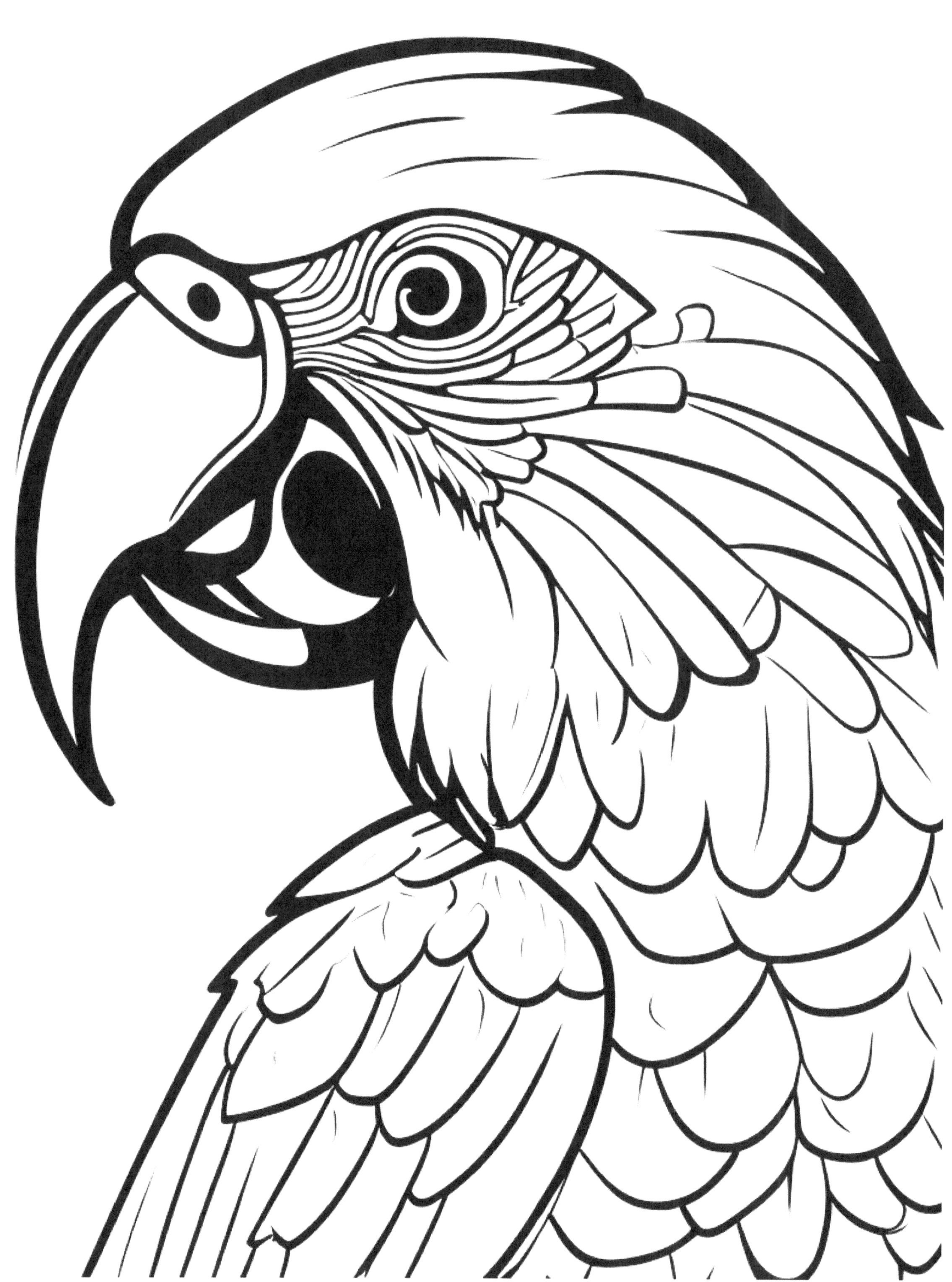

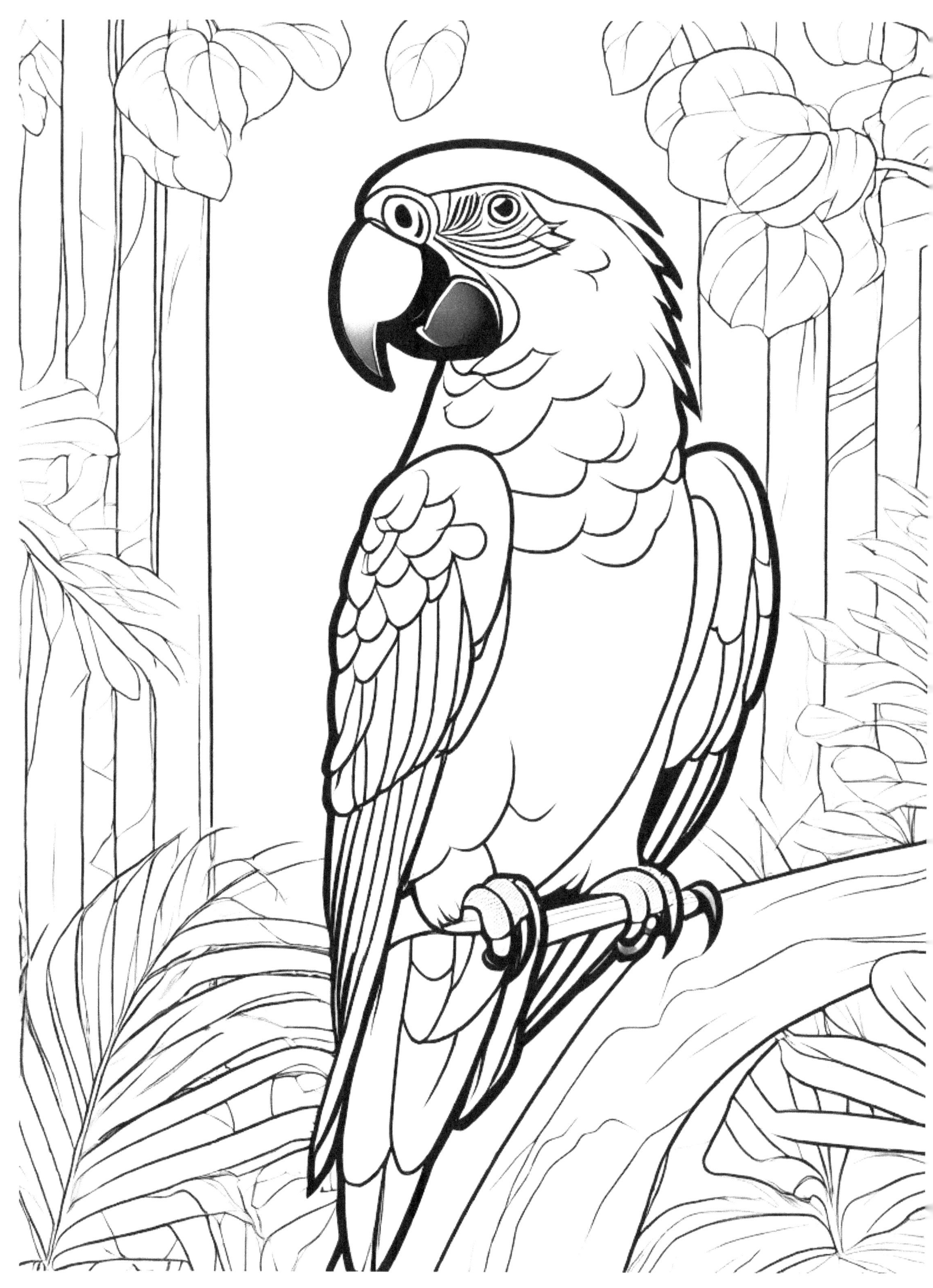

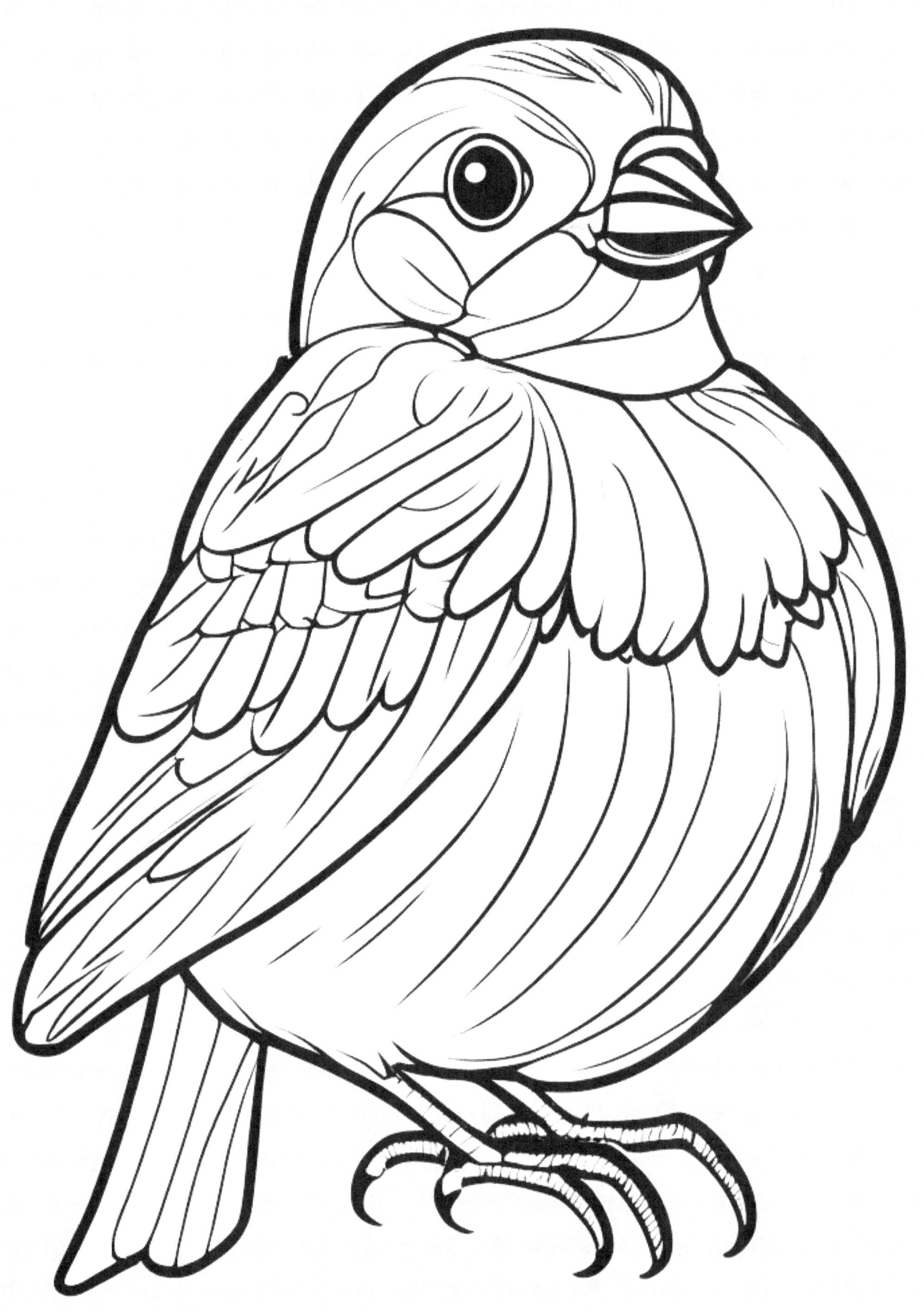

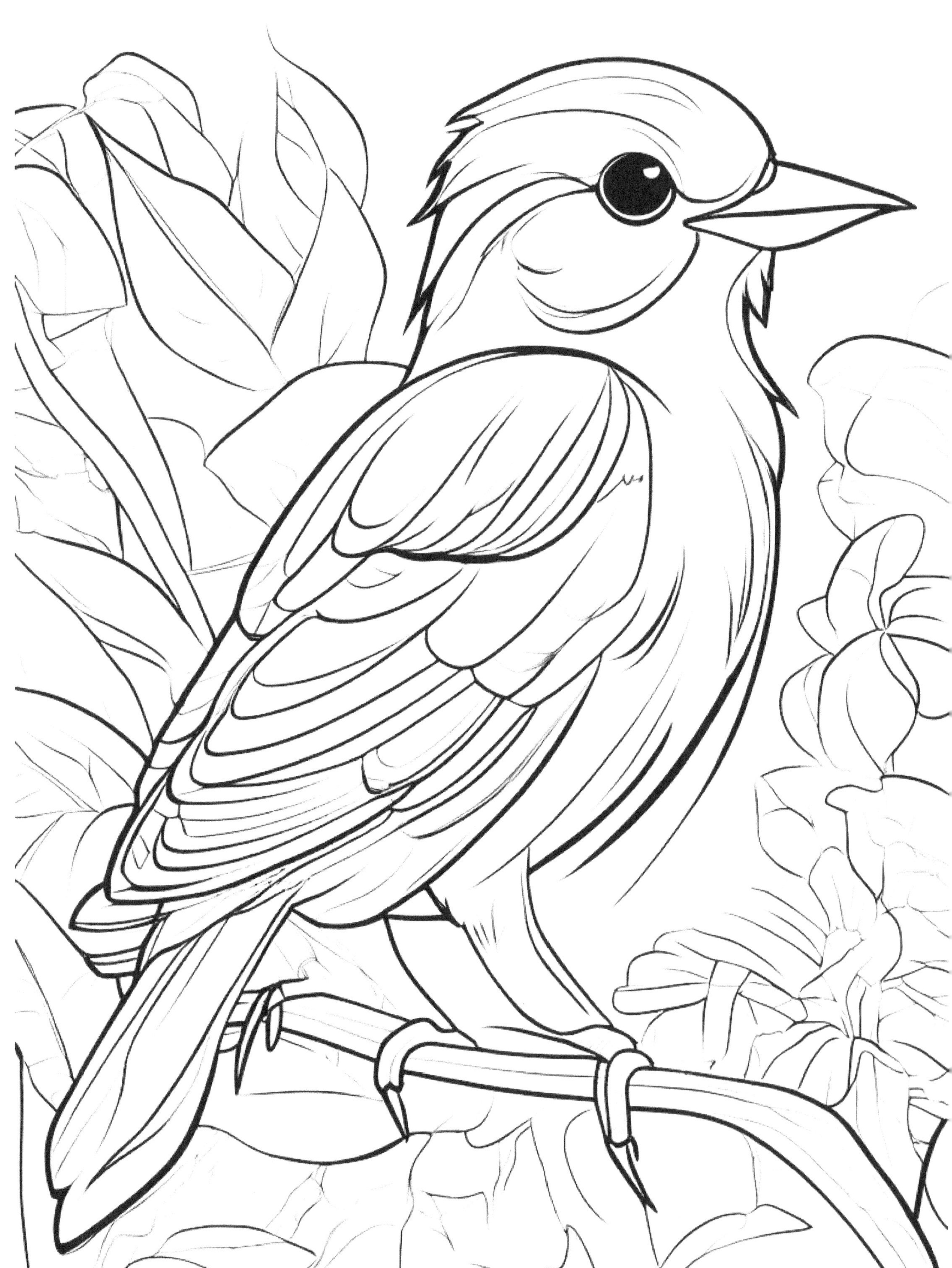

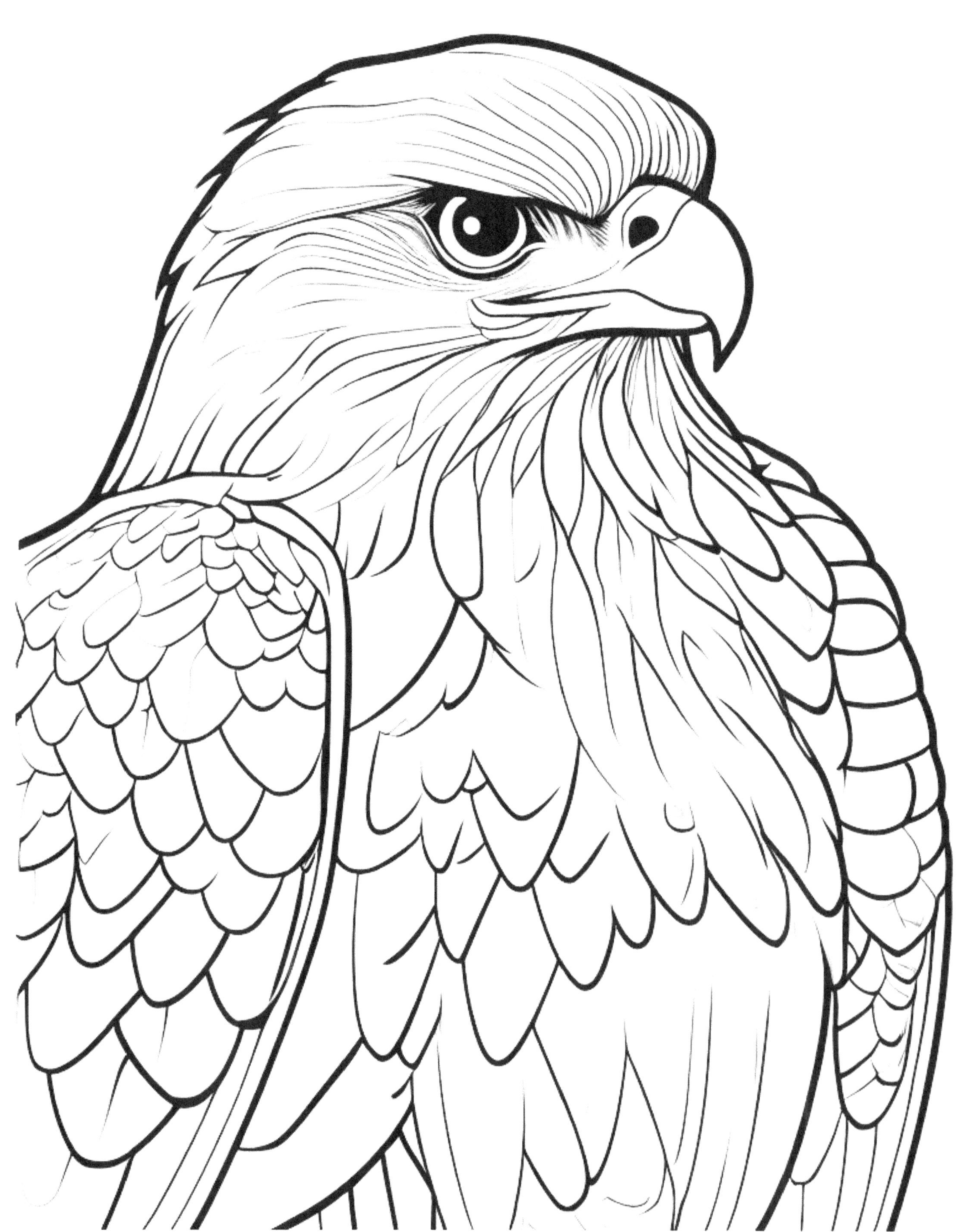

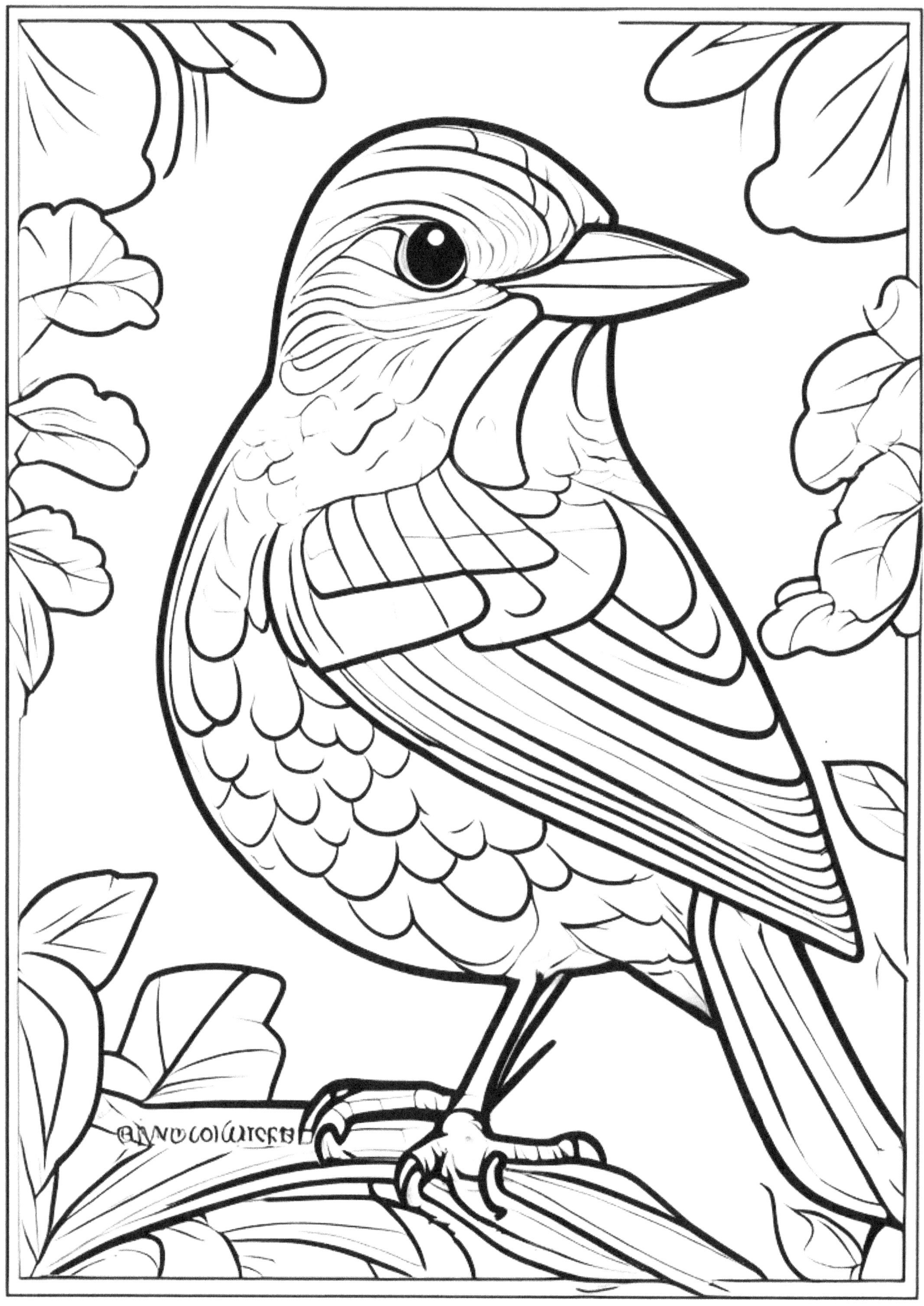

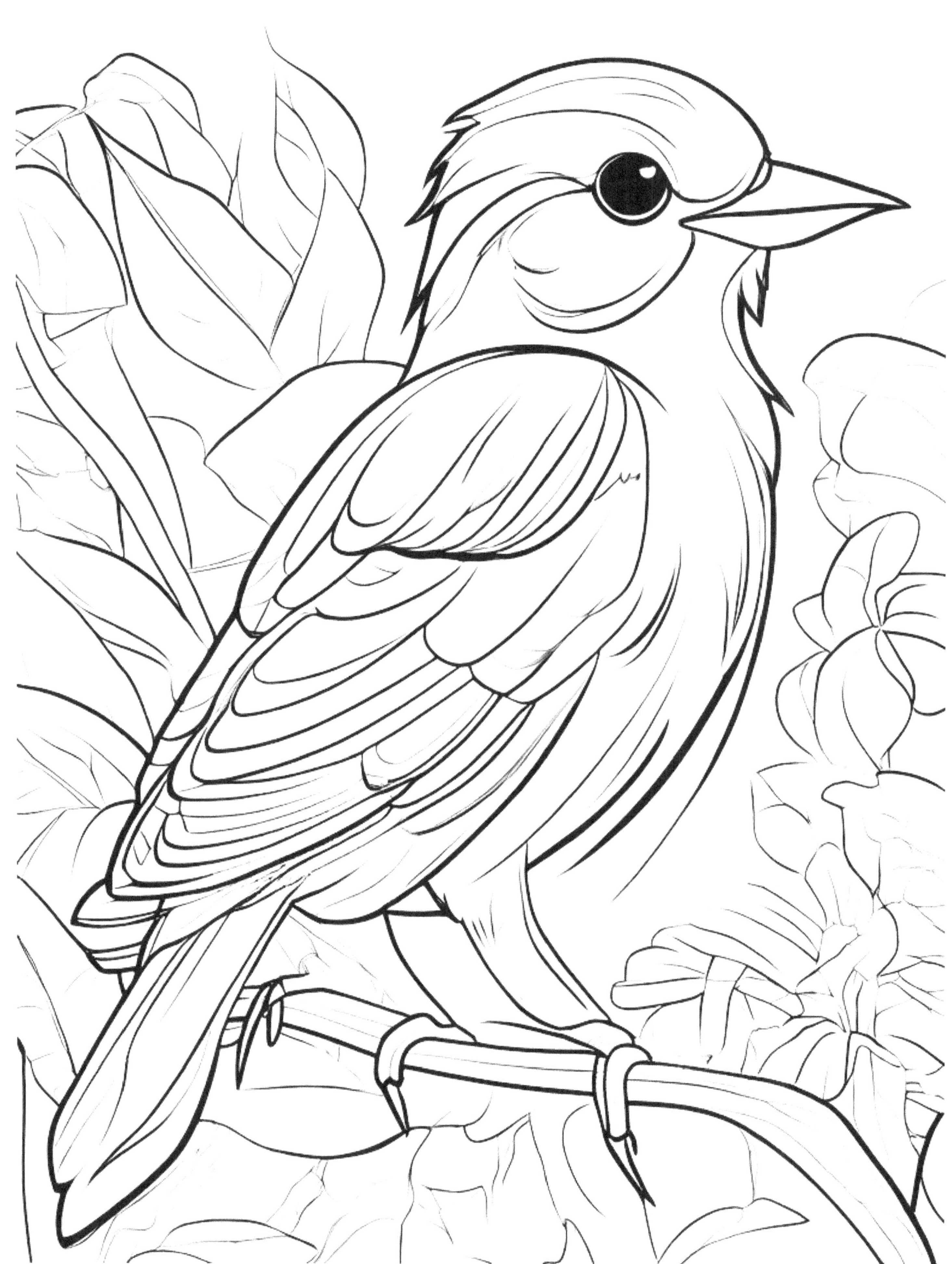

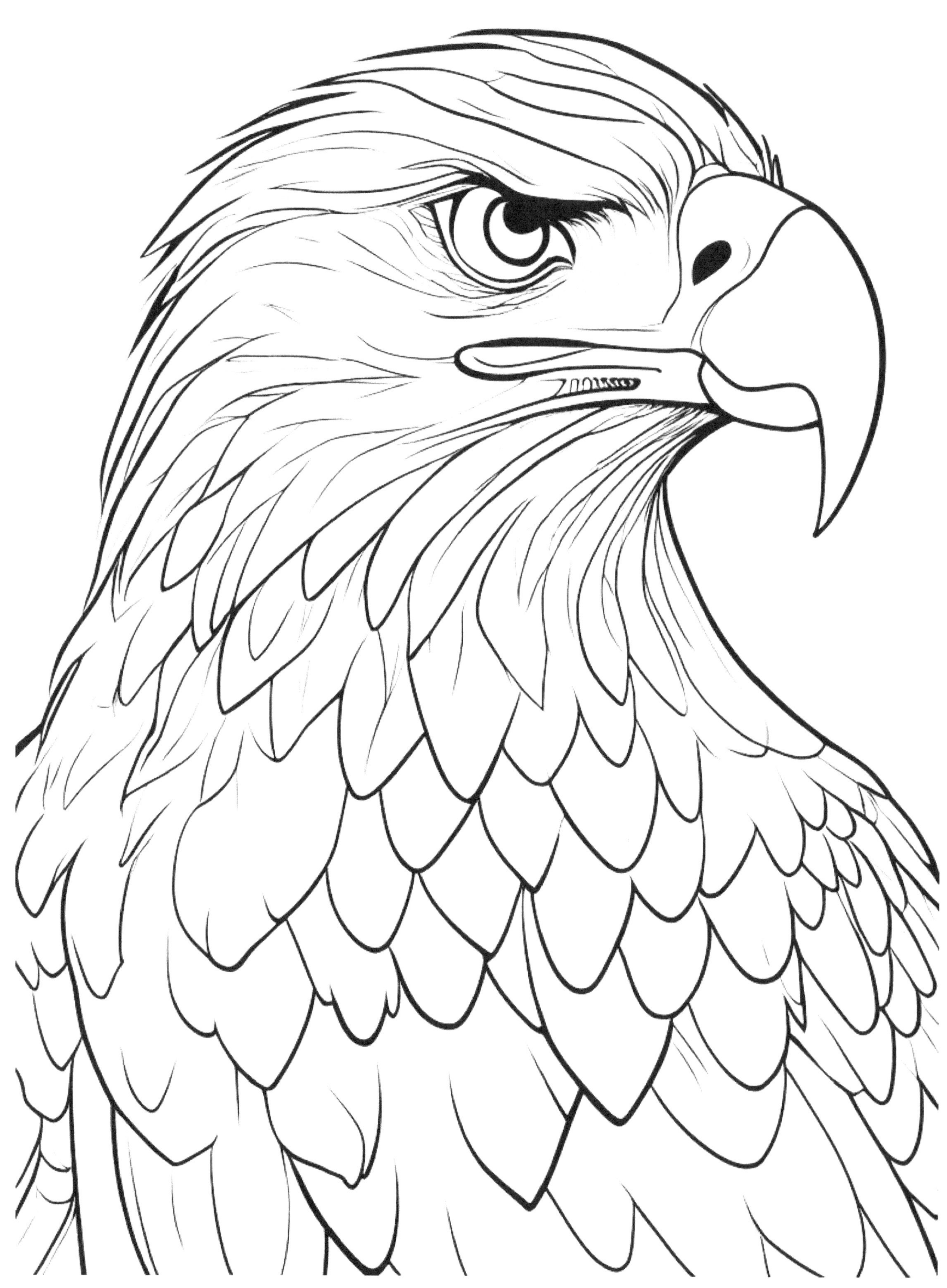

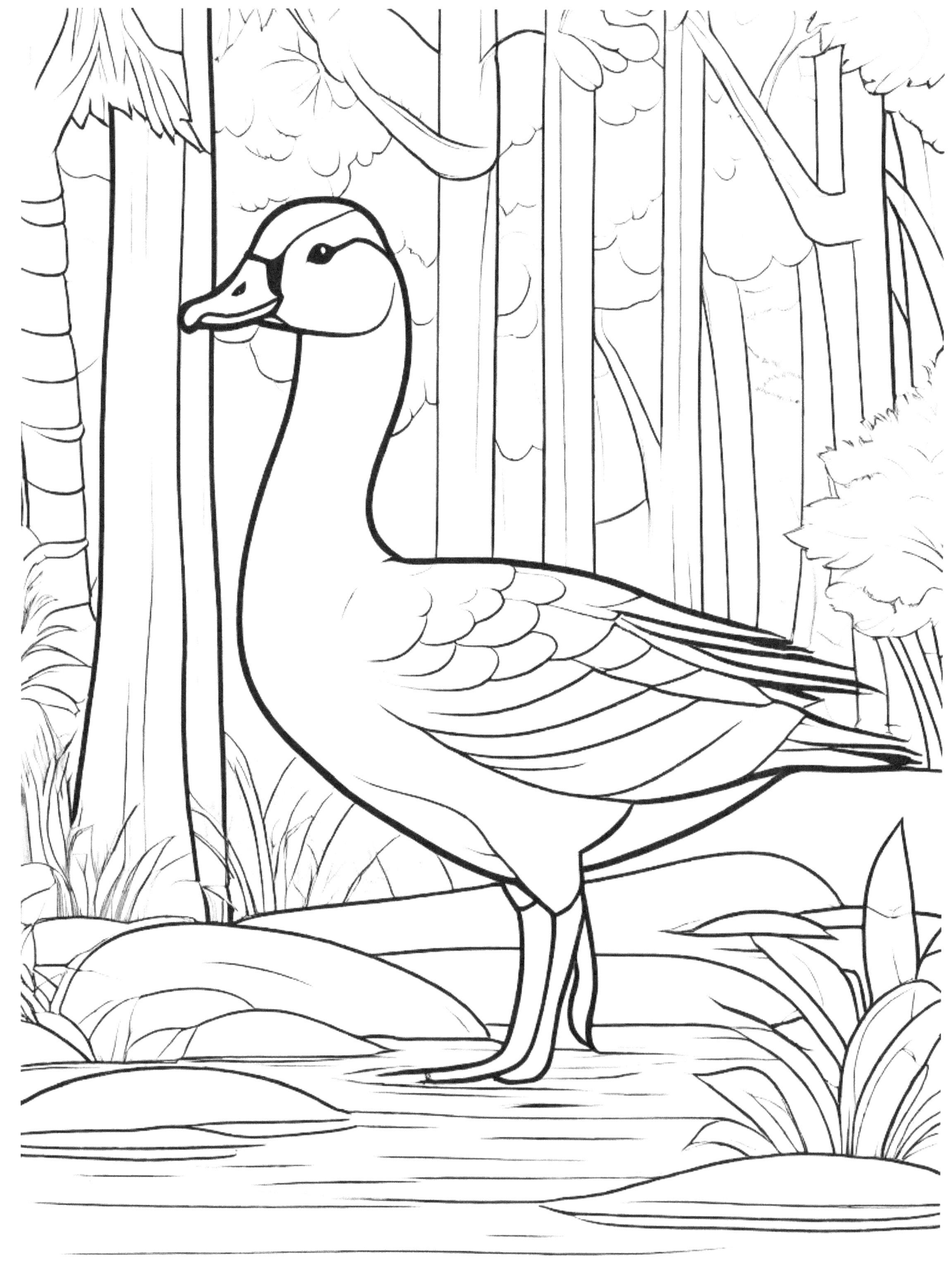

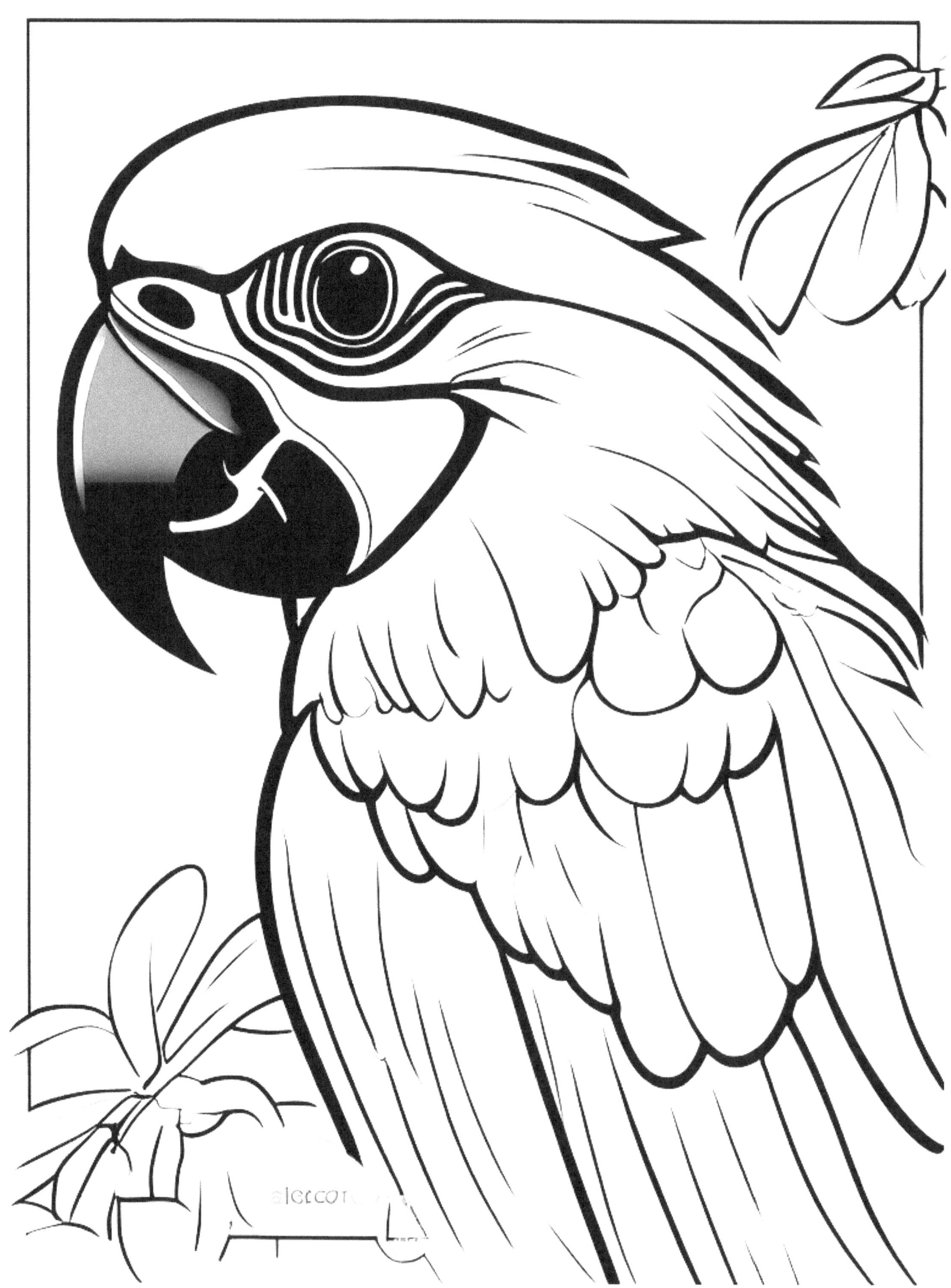

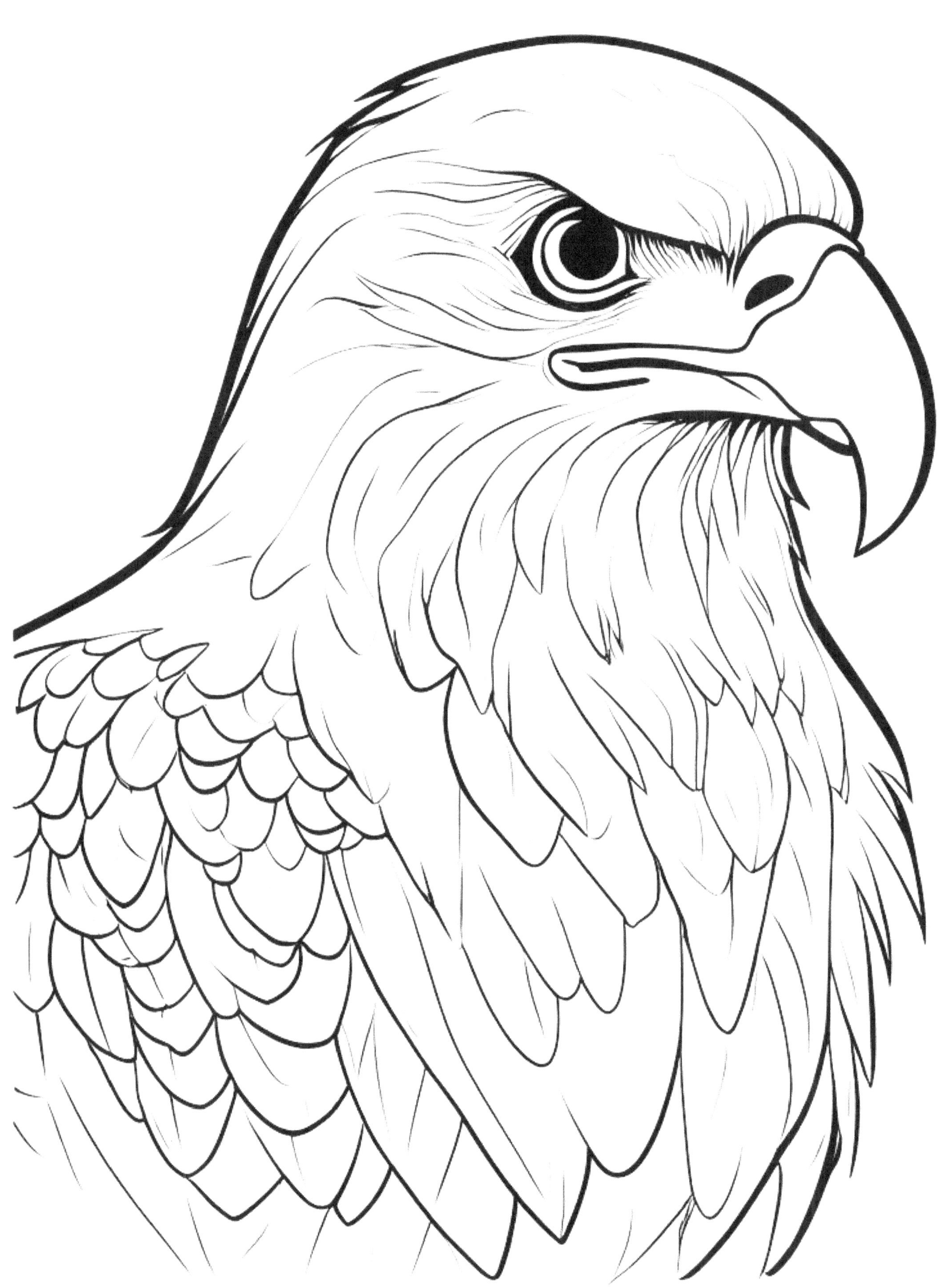

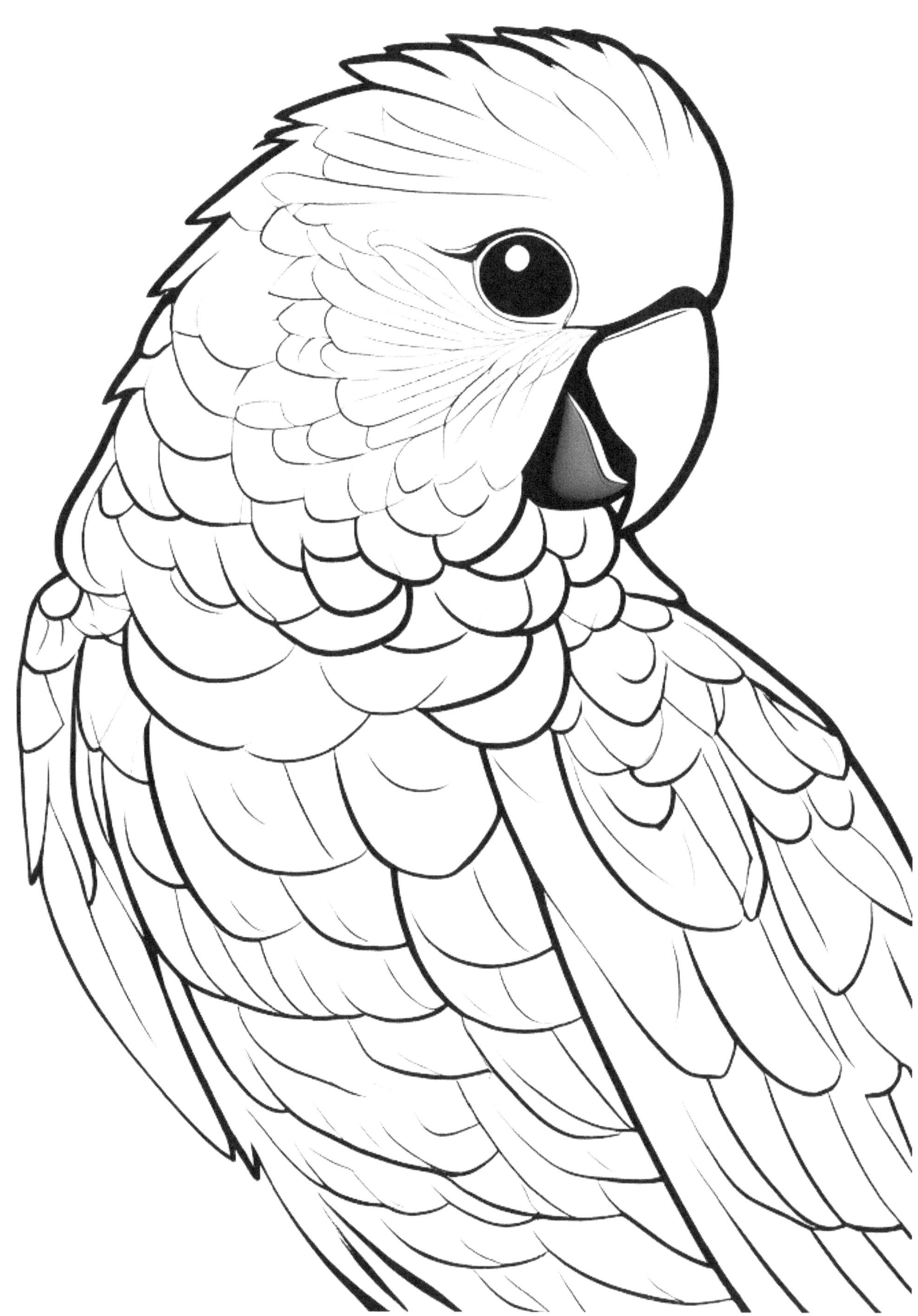

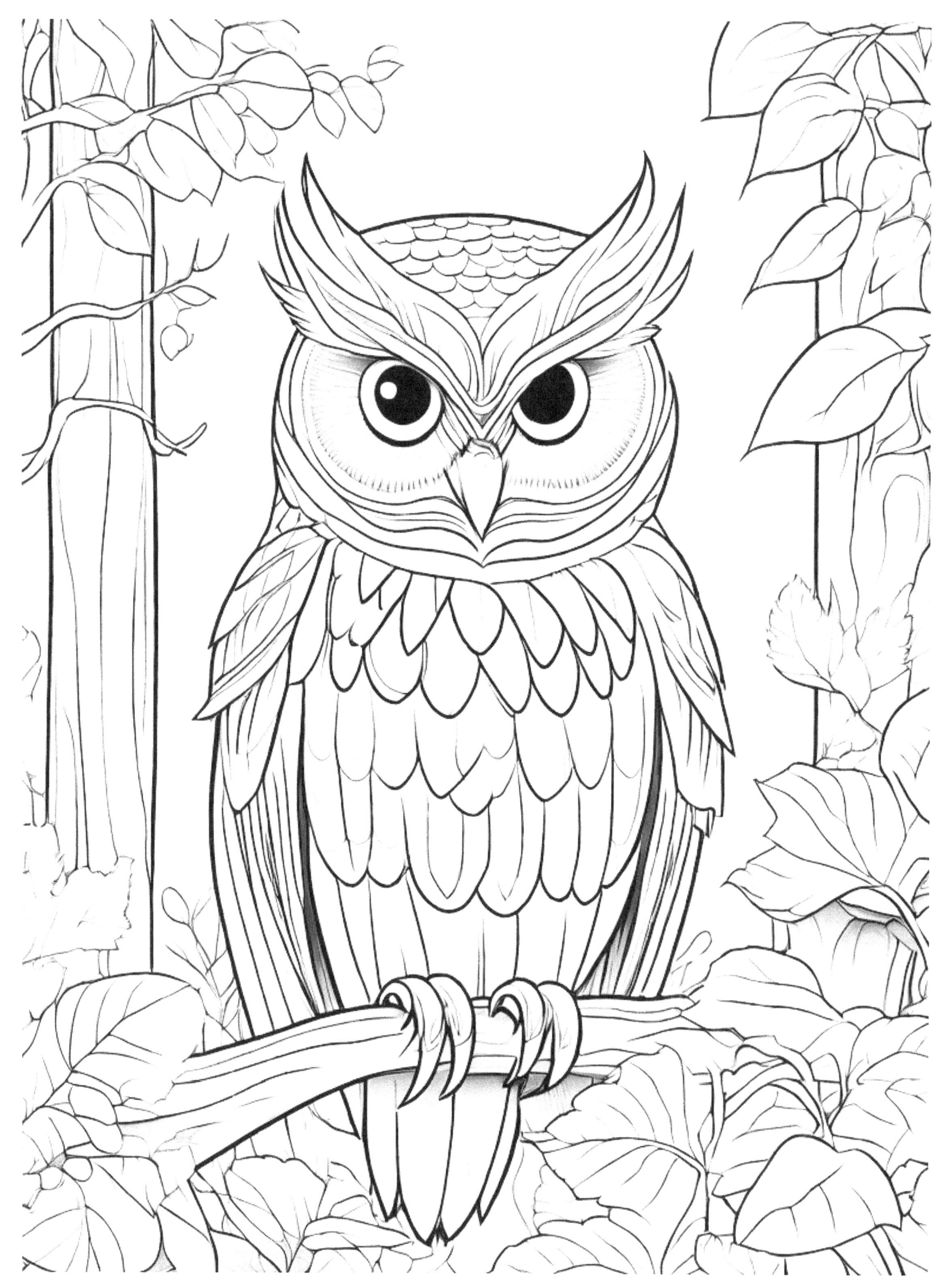

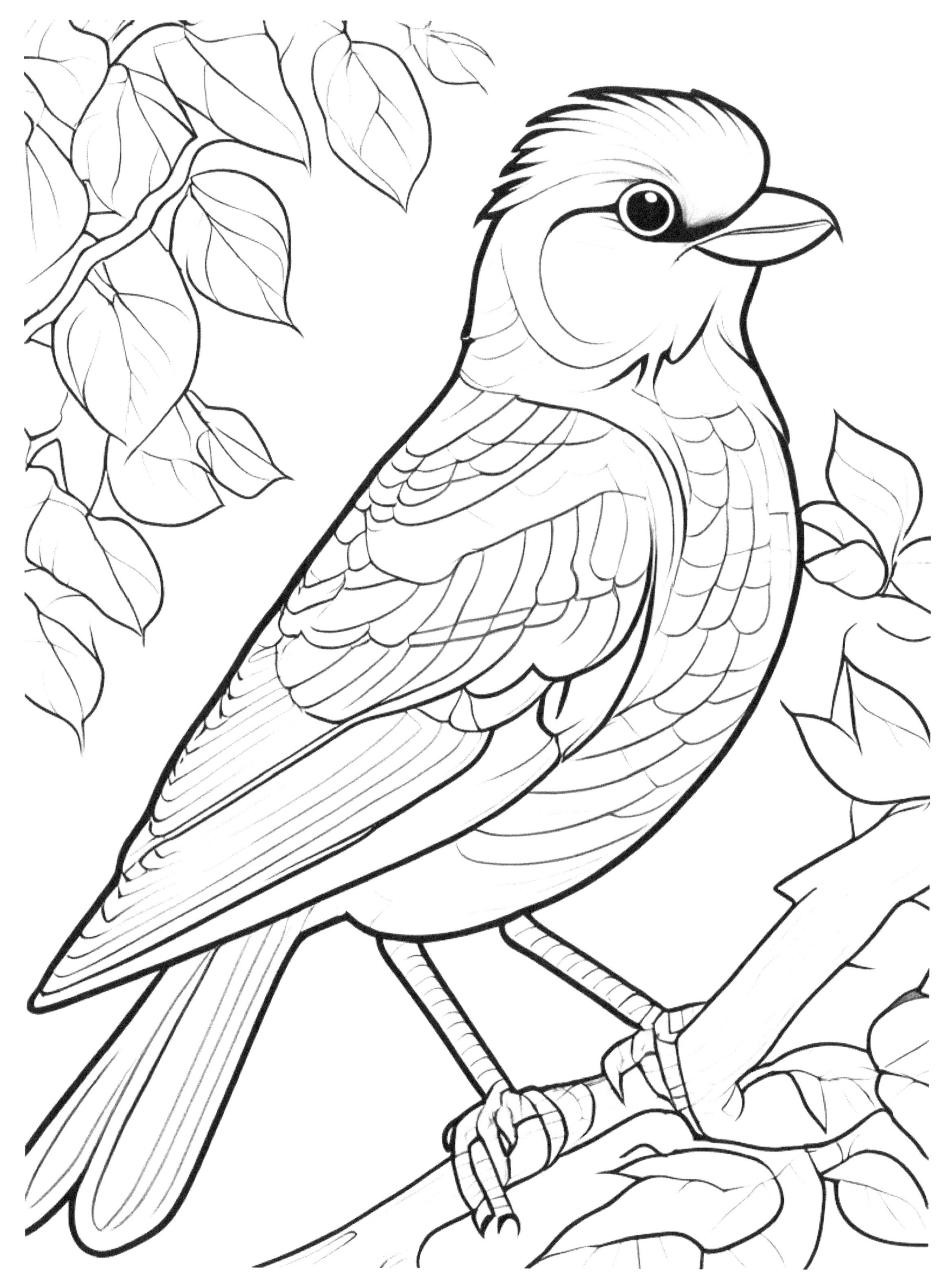